FREE Test Taking Tips DVD Offer

To help us better serve you, we have developed a Test Taking Tips DVD that we would like to give you for FREE. **This DVD covers world-class test taking tips that you can use to be even more successful when you are taking your test.**

All that we ask is that you email us your feedback about your study guide. Please let us know what you thought about it – whether that is good, bad or indifferent.

To get your **FREE Test Taking Tips DVD**, email freedvd@studyguideteam.com with "FREE DVD" in the subject line and the following information in the body of the email:

a. The title of your study guide.

b. Your product rating on a scale of 1-5, with 5 being the highest rating.

c. Your feedback about the study guide. What did you think of it?

d. Your full name and shipping address to send your free DVD.

If you have any questions or concerns, please don't hesitate to contact us at freedvd@studyguideteam.com.

Thanks again!

SAT Reading and Writing Prep Study Guide & Practice Test Questions for the SAT Reading Comprehension, SAT Writing and Language, and SAT Essay Sections

Test Prep Books

Table of Contents

Quick Overview

As you draw closer to taking your exam, effective preparation becomes more and more important. Thankfully, you have this study guide to help you get ready. Use this guide to help keep your studying on track and refer to it often.

This study guide contains several key sections that will help you be successful on your exam. The guide contains tips for what you should do the night before and the day of the test. Also included are test-taking tips. Knowing the right information is not always enough. Many well-prepared test takers struggle with exams. These tips will help equip you to accurately read, assess, and answer test questions.

A large part of the guide is devoted to showing you what content to expect on the exam and to helping you better understand that content. In this guide are practice test questions so that you can see how well you have grasped the content. Then, answer explanations are provided so that you can understand why you missed certain questions.

Don't try to cram the night before you take your exam. This is not a wise strategy for a few reasons. First, your retention of the information will be low. Your time would be better used by reviewing information you already know rather than trying to learn a lot of new information. Second, you will likely become stressed as you try to gain a large amount of knowledge in a short amount of time. Third, you will be depriving yourself of sleep. So be sure to go to bed at a reasonable time the night before. Being well-rested helps you focus and remain calm.

Be sure to eat a substantial breakfast the morning of the exam. If you are taking the exam in the afternoon, be sure to have a good lunch as well. Being hungry is distracting and can make it difficult to focus. You have hopefully spent lots of time preparing for the exam. Don't let an empty stomach get in the way of success!

When travelling to the testing center, leave earlier than needed. That way, you have a buffer in case you experience any delays. This will help you remain calm and will keep you from missing your appointment time at the testing center.

Be sure to pace yourself during the exam. Don't try to rush through the exam. There is no need to risk performing poorly on the exam just so you can leave the testing center early. Allow yourself to use all of the allotted time if needed.

Remain positive while taking the exam even if you feel like you are performing poorly. Thinking about the content you should have mastered will not help you perform better on the exam.

Once the exam is complete, take some time to relax. Even if you feel that you need to take the exam again, you will be well served by some down time before you begin studying again. It's often easier to convince yourself to study if you know that it will come with a reward!

Test-Taking Strategies

1. Predicting the Answer

When you feel confident in your preparation for a multiple-choice test, try predicting the answer before reading the answer choices. This is especially useful on questions that test objective factual knowledge. By predicting the answer before reading the available choices, you eliminate the possibility that you will be distracted or led astray by an incorrect answer choice. You will feel more confident in your selection if you read the question, predict the answer, and then find your prediction among the answer choices. After using this strategy, be sure to still read all of the answer choices carefully and completely. If you feel unprepared, you should not attempt to predict the answers. This would be a waste of time and an opportunity for your mind to wander in the wrong direction.

2. Reading the Whole Question

Too often, test takers scan a multiple-choice question, recognize a few familiar words, and immediately jump to the answer choices. Test authors are aware of this common impatience, and they will sometimes prey upon it. For instance, a test author might subtly turn the question into a negative, or he or she might redirect the focus of the question right at the end. The only way to avoid falling into these traps is to read the entirety of the question carefully before reading the answer choices.

3. Looking for Wrong Answers

Long and complicated multiple-choice questions can be intimidating. One way to simplify a difficult multiple-choice question is to eliminate all of the answer choices that are clearly wrong. In most sets of answers, there will be at least one selection that can be dismissed right away. If the test is administered on paper, the test taker could draw a line through it to indicate that it may be ignored; otherwise, the test taker will have to perform this operation mentally or on scratch paper. In either case, once the obviously incorrect answers have been eliminated, the remaining choices may be considered. Sometimes identifying the clearly wrong answers will give the test taker some information about the correct answer. For instance, if one of the remaining answer choices is a direct opposite of one of the eliminated answer choices, it may well be the correct answer. The opposite of obviously wrong is obviously right! Of course, this is not always the case. Some answers are obviously incorrect simply because they are irrelevant to the question being asked. Still, identifying and eliminating some incorrect answer choices is a good way to simplify a multiple-choice question.

4. Don't Overanalyze

Anxious test takers often overanalyze questions. When you are nervous, your brain will often run wild, causing you to make associations and discover clues that don't actually exist. If you feel that this may be a problem for you, do whatever you can to slow down during the test. Try taking a deep breath or counting to ten. As you read and consider the question, restrict yourself to the particular words used by the author. Avoid thought tangents about what the author *really* meant, or what he or she was *trying* to say. The only things that matter on a multiple-choice test are the words that are actually in the question. You must avoid reading too much into a multiple-choice question, or supposing that the writer meant something other than what he or she wrote.

5. No Need for Panic

It is wise to learn as many strategies as possible before taking a multiple-choice test, but it is likely that you will come across a few questions for which you simply don't know the answer. In this situation, avoid panicking. Because most multiple-choice tests include dozens of questions, the relative value of a single wrong answer is small. As much as possible, you should compartmentalize each question on a multiple-choice test. In other words, you should not allow your feelings about one question to affect your success on the others. When you find a question that you either don't understand or don't know how to answer, just take a deep breath and do your best. Read the entire question slowly and carefully. Try rephrasing the question a couple of different ways. Then, read all of the answer choices carefully. After eliminating obviously wrong answers, make a selection and move on to the next question.

6. Confusing Answer Choices

When working on a difficult multiple-choice question, there may be a tendency to focus on the answer choices that are the easiest to understand. Many people, whether consciously or not, gravitate to the answer choices that require the least concentration, knowledge, and memory. This is a mistake. When you come across an answer choice that is confusing, you should give it extra attention. A question might be confusing because you do not know the subject matter to which it refers. If this is the case, don't eliminate the answer before you have affirmatively settled on another. When you come across an answer choice of this type, set it aside as you look at the remaining choices. If you can confidently assert that one of the other choices is correct, you can leave the confusing answer aside. Otherwise, you will need to take a moment to try to better understand the confusing answer choice. Rephrasing is one way to tease out the sense of a confusing answer choice.

7. Your First Instinct

Many people struggle with multiple-choice tests because they overthink the questions. If you have studied sufficiently for the test, you should be prepared to trust your first instinct once you have carefully and completely read the question and all of the answer choices. There is a great deal of research suggesting that the mind can come to the correct conclusion very quickly once it has obtained all of the relevant information. At times, it may seem to you as if your intuition is working faster even than your reasoning mind. This may in fact be true. The knowledge you obtain while studying may be retrieved from your subconscious before you have a chance to work out the associations that support it. Verify your instinct by working out the reasons that it should be trusted.

8. Key Words

Many test takers struggle with multiple-choice questions because they have poor reading comprehension skills. Quickly reading and understanding a multiple-choice question requires a mixture of skill and experience. To help with this, try jotting down a few key words and phrases on a piece of scrap paper. Doing this concentrates the process of reading and forces the mind to weigh the relative importance of the question's parts. In selecting words and phrases to write down, the test taker thinks about the question more deeply and carefully. This is especially true for multiple-choice questions that are preceded by a long prompt.

9. Subtle Negatives

One of the oldest tricks in the multiple-choice test writer's book is to subtly reverse the meaning of a question with a word like *not* or *except*. If you are not paying attention to each word in the question, you can easily be led astray by this trick. For instance, a common question format is, "Which of the following is...?" Obviously, if the question instead is, "Which of the following is not...?," then the answer will be quite different. Even worse, the test makers are aware of the potential for this mistake and will include one answer choice that would be correct if the question were not negated or reversed. A test taker who misses the reversal will find what he or she believes to be a correct answer and will be so confident that he or she will fail to reread the question and discover the original error. The only way to avoid this is to practice a wide variety of multiple-choice questions and to pay close attention to each and every word.

10. Reading Every Answer Choice

It may seem obvious, but you should always read every one of the answer choices! Too many test takers fall into the habit of scanning the question and assuming that they understand the question because they recognize a few key words. From there, they pick the first answer choice that answers the question they believe they have read. Test takers who read all of the answer choices might discover that one of the latter answer choices is actually *more* correct. Moreover, reading all of the answer choices can remind you of facts related to the question that can help you arrive at the correct answer. Sometimes, a misstatement or incorrect detail in one of the latter answer choices will trigger your memory of the subject and will enable you to find the right answer. Failing to read all of the answer choices is like not reading all of the items on a restaurant menu: you might miss out on the perfect choice.

11. Spot the Hedges

One of the keys to success on multiple-choice tests is paying close attention to every word. This is never truer than with words like almost, most, some, and sometimes. These words are called "hedges" because they indicate that a statement is not totally true or not true in every place and time. An absolute statement will contain no hedges, but in many subjects, the answers are not always straightforward or absolute. There are always exceptions to the rules in these subjects. For this reason, you should favor those multiple-choice questions that contain hedging language. The presence of qualifying words indicates that the author is taking special care with his or her words, which is certainly important when composing the right answer. After all, there are many ways to be wrong, but there is only one way to be right! For this reason, it is wise to avoid answers that are absolute when taking a multiple-choice test. An absolute answer is one that says things are either all one way or all another. They often include words like *every*, *always*, *best*, and *never*. If you are taking a multiple-choice test in a subject that doesn't lend itself to absolute answers, be on your guard if you see any of these words.

12. Long Answers

In many subject areas, the answers are not simple. As already mentioned, the right answer often requires hedges. Another common feature of the answers to a complex or subjective question are qualifying clauses, which are groups of words that subtly modify the meaning of the sentence. If the question or answer choice describes a rule to which there are exceptions or the subject matter is complicated, ambiguous, or confusing, the correct answer will require many words in order to be expressed clearly and accurately. In essence, you should not be deterred by answer choices that seem excessively long. Oftentimes, the author of the text will not be able to write the correct answer without offering some qualifications and modifications. Your job is to read the answer choices thoroughly and completely and to select the one that most accurately and precisely answers the question.

13. Restating to Understand

Sometimes, a question on a multiple-choice test is difficult not because of what it asks but because of how it is written. If this is the case, restate the question or answer choice in different words. This process serves a couple of important purposes. First, it forces you to concentrate on the core of the question. In order to rephrase the question accurately, you have to understand it well. Rephrasing the question will concentrate your mind on the key words and ideas. Second, it will present the information to your mind in a fresh way. This process may trigger your memory and render some useful scrap of information picked up while studying.

14. True Statements

Sometimes an answer choice will be true in itself, but it does not answer the question. This is one of the main reasons why it is essential to read the question carefully and completely before proceeding to the answer choices. Too often, test takers skip ahead to the answer choices and look for true statements. Having found one of these, they are content to select it without reference to the question above. Obviously, this provides an easy way for test makers to play tricks. The savvy test taker will always read the entire question before turning to the answer choices. Then, having settled on a correct answer choice, he or she will refer to the original question and ensure that the selected answer is relevant. The mistake of choosing a correct-but-irrelevant answer choice is especially common on questions related to specific pieces of objective knowledge. A prepared test taker will have a wealth of factual knowledge at his or her disposal, and should not be careless in its application.

15. No Patterns

One of the more dangerous ideas that circulates about multiple-choice tests is that the correct answers tend to fall into patterns. These erroneous ideas range from a belief that B and C are the most common right answers, to the idea that an unprepared test-taker should answer "A-B-A-C-A-D-A-B-A." It cannot be emphasized enough that pattern-seeking of this type is exactly the WRONG way to approach a multiple-choice test. To begin with, it is highly unlikely that the test maker will plot the correct answers according to some predetermined pattern. The questions are scrambled and delivered in a random order. Furthermore, even if the test maker was following a pattern in the assignation of correct answers, there is no reason why the test taker would know which pattern he or she was using. Any attempt to discern a pattern in the answer choices is a waste of time and a distraction from the real work of taking the test. A test taker would be much better served by extra preparation before the test than by reliance on a pattern in the answers.

FREE DVD OFFER

Don't forget that doing well on your exam includes both understanding the test content and understanding how to use what you know to do well on the test. We offer a completely FREE Test Taking Tips DVD that covers world class test taking tips that you can use to be even more successful when you are taking your test.

All that we ask is that you email us your feedback about your study guide. To get your **FREE Test Taking Tips DVD**, email freedvd@studyguideteam.com with "FREE DVD" in the subject line and the following information in the body of the email:

- The title of your study guide.
- Your product rating on a scale of 1-5, with 5 being the highest rating.
- Your feedback about the study guide. What did you think of it?
- Your full name and shipping address to send your free DVD.

Introduction to the SAT

Function of the Test

The SAT is a standardized test taken by high school students across the United States and given internationally for college placement. It is designed to measure problem solving ability, communication, and understanding complex relationships. The SAT also serves as a qualifying measure to identify students for college scholarships, depending on the college being applied to. All colleges in the U.S. accept the SAT, and, in addition to admissions and scholarships, use SAT scores for course placement as well as academic counseling.

Most of the high school students who take the SAT are seniors. In 2016, the number of students who took the SAT was just under 1.7 million. It's important to note that since many updates have been implemented during the 2016 year, the data points cannot be compared to those in previous years. In 2014, 42.6 percent of students met the College Board's "college and career readiness" benchmark, and in 2015, 41.9 percent met this benchmark.

Test Administration

The SAT is offered on seven days throughout the year at schools throughout the United States. Internationally, the SAT is offered on five days throughout the year. There are thousands of testing centers worldwide. Test-takers can view the test centers in their area when they register for the test, or they can view testing locations at the College Board website, a not-for-profit that owns and publishes the SAT.

The SAT registration fee is $46, and the SAT with Essay registration fee is $60, although both of these have fee waivers available. Also note that students outside the U.S. may have to pay an extra processing fee. Additional fees include registering by phone, changing fee, late registration fee, or a waitlist fee. Test-takers may register four score reports for free up to nine days after the test. Any additional score reports cost $12, although fee waivers are available for this as well.

Test Format

The SAT gauges a student's proficiency in three areas: Reading, Mathematics, and Writing and Language. The reading portion of the SAT measures comprehension, requiring candidates to read multi-paragraph fiction and non-fiction segments including informational visuals, such as charts, tables and graphs, and answer questions based on this content. Fluency in problem solving, conceptual understanding of equations, and real-world applications are characteristics of the math test. The writing and language portion requires students to evaluate and edit writing and graphics to obtain an answer that correctly conveys the information given in the passage.

The SAT contains 154 multiple-choice questions, with each section comprising over 40 questions. A different length of time is given for each section, for a total of three hours, plus fifty minutes for the essay (optional).

Section	**Time (In Minutes)**	**Number of Questions**
Reading	65	52
Writing and Language	35	44
Mathematics	80	58
Essay (optional)	50 (optional)	1 (optional)
Total	**180**	**154**

Scoring

Scores for the new SAT are based on a scale from 400 to 1600. Scores range from 200 to 800 for Evidence-Based Reading and Writing, and 200 to 800 for Math. The optional essay is scored from 2 to 8. The SAT also no longer penalizes for incorrect answers. Therefore, a student's raw score is the number of correctly answered questions.

On the College Board website, there are indicators to determine what the benchmark scores are. The scores are divided up into green, yellow, or red. Green meets or exceeds the benchmark, and shows a 480 to 800 in Evidence-Based Reading and Writing, and a 530 to 800 in Math.

Recent/Future Developments

The SAT taken before March 2016 is different than the one administered currently. Currently, the essay is optional, and the time limit for the Reading, Writing, and Math sections has increased per section. The content features also vary, with the new test focusing on skills that research has identified as most important for college readiness and the meaning of words in extended context rather than emphasis on vocabulary. The score range has changed from 600–2400 to 400–1600. There has also been added subscore reporting, which provides insight to students and parents about the scores.

Reading

The Reading section of the SAT measures test takers' ability to read, understand, and interpret the types of texts they will encounter in higher education and their vocational pursuits. The passages included in this section are drawn from previously-published literary or informational texts. Some passages include graphics such as charts, graphs, and tables, which the test taker must interpret alongside the written text to correctly answer the questions. Other questions will follow two passages that are purposely paired for the test taker to compare and contrast.

The Reading section contains 65 questions, which must be answered in the allotted 52 minutes. The majority of the passages in this section are pulled from informational or nonfiction works, covering topics pertaining to history, humanities, science, and social studies. At least one single passage or a pair of passages to be considered together will be drawn from the seminal founding U.S. documents or the *Great Global Conversation,* which is an umbrella term used to describe works from countries around the world and spanning several centuries that address universal topics like justice, freedom, and human dignity. Test takers will encounter only one literary passage in the Reading Section. This except is drawn from an American or international fictional piece, such as a published novel or short story.

In addition to encountering a variety of topics in the passages, test takers will need to employ their comprehension skills pertaining to understanding texts written for different purposes. Some texts may tell a story or describe a process. Others will present an argument and support for an opinion, while still other passages may delineate the purpose of a study or experiment. The text complexity or reading level of each passage also varies; passages may span the gamut from a ninth-grade reading level to that expected of a first-year university student or post-secondary scholar.

Questions on the Reading section will generally fall into one of three principle categories: information and ideas, rhetoric, and synthesis. As the name implies, information and ideas questions focus on the direct or indirect ideas or facts that the passage presents. The answers to some of these questions will not necessarily be explicitly revealed in the passage; rather, test takers must use their inferential skills to uncover the author's implied meaning. Rhetoric questions require test takers to consider the method or manner in which the author conveys his or her intended message. Lastly, synthesis questions ask test takers to draw conclusions from a passage or make connections between a pair of passages or between passages and an accompanying graphic.

While the vast majority of questions in the Reading section address the test taker's ability to understand written language and ideas in each passage, a small number of questions will also assess the test taker's ability to interpret graph, tables, and charts. For this reason, in addition to studying reading comprehension techniques and honing skills related to synthesis and inference, test takers should practice reading and interpreting tables, graphs, and charts. Test takers should review the material in this section pertaining to critical reading skills and refer to the information in the Writing and Language section about specific comprehension skills pertinent to history and the sciences texts, as well as graphic-interpreting techniques.

Command of Evidence

Command of evidence, or the ability to use contextual clues, factual statements, and corroborative phrases to support an author's message or intent, is an important part of the Reading section of the SAT. A test taker's ability to parse out factual information and draw conclusions based on evidence is important to critical reading comprehension. The test will ask students to read text passages, and then answer questions based on information contained in them. These types of questions may ask test takers to identify stated facts. They may also require test takers to draw logical conclusions, identify data based on graphs, make inferences, and to generally display analytical thinking skills.

Finding Evidence in a Passage

The basic tenant of reading comprehension is the ability to read and understand text. One way to understand text is to look for information that supports the author's main idea, topic, or position statement. This information may be factual or it may be based on the author's opinion. This section will focus on the test taker's ability to identify factual information, as opposed to opinionated bias. The Reading section will ask test takers to read passages containing factual information, and then logically relate those passages by drawing conclusions based on evidence.

In order to identify factual information within a text passage, test takers should begin by looking for statements of fact. Factual statements can be either true or false. Identifying factual statements as opposed to opinion statements is important in demonstrating full command of evidence in reading. For example, the statement *The temperature outside was unbearably hot* may seem like a fact; however, it's not. While anyone can point to a temperature gauge as factual evidence, the statement itself reflects only an opinion. Some people may find the temperature unbearably hot. Others may find it comfortably warm. Thus, the sentence, *The temperature outside was unbearably hot,* reflects the opinion of the author who found it unbearable. If the text passage followed up the sentence with atmospheric conditions indicating heat indices above 140 degrees Fahrenheit, then the reader knows there is factual information that supports the author's assertion of *unbearably hot*.

In looking for information that can be proven or disproven, it's helpful to scan for dates, numbers, timelines, equations, statistics, and other similar data within any given text passage. These types of indicators will point to proven particulars. For example, the statement, *The temperature outside was unbearably hot on that summer day, July 10, 1913,* most likely indicates factual information, even if the reader is unaware that this is the hottest day on record in the United States. Be careful when reading biased words from an author. Biased words indicate opinion, as opposed to fact. See the list of biased words below and keep in mind that it's not an inclusive list:

- Good/bad
- Great/greatest
- Better/best/worst
- Amazing
- Terrible/bad/awful
- Beautiful/handsome/ugly
- More/most
- Exciting/dull/boring
- Favorite
- Very
- Probably/should/seem/possibly

Remember, most of what is written is actually opinion or carefully worded information that seems like fact when it isn't. To say, *duplicating DNA results is not cost-effective* sounds like it could be a scientific fact, but it isn't. Factual information can be verified through independent sources.

The simplest type of test question may provide a text passage, then ask the test taker to distinguish the correct factual supporting statement that best answers the corresponding question on the test. However, be aware that most questions may ask the test taker to read more than one text passage and identify which answer best supports an author's topic. While the ability to identify factual information is critical, these types of questions require the test taker to identify chunks of details, and then relate them to one another.

Displaying Analytical Thinking Skills

Analytical thinking involves being able to break down visual information into manageable portions in order to solve complex problems or process difficult concepts. This skill encompasses all aspects of command of evidence in reading comprehension.

A reader can approach analytical thinking in a series of steps. First, when approaching visual material, a reader should identify an author's thought process. Is the line of reasoning clear from the presented passage, or does it require inference and coming to a conclusion independent of the author? Next, a reader should evaluate the author's line of reasoning to determine if the logic is sound. Look for evidentiary clues and cited sources. Do these hold up under the author's argument? Third, look for bias. Bias includes generalized, emotional statements that will not hold up under scrutiny, as they are not based on fact. From there, a reader should ask if the presented evidence is trustworthy. Are the facts cited from reliable sources? Are they current? Is there any new factual information that has come to light since the passage was written that renders the argument useless? Next, a reader should carefully think about information that opposes the author's view. Do the author's arguments guide the reader to identical thoughts, or is there room for sound arguments? Finally, a reader should always be able to identify an author's conclusion and be able to weigh its effectiveness.

The ability to display analytical thinking skills while reading is key in any standardized testing situation. Test takers should be able to critically evaluate the information provided, and then answer questions related to content by using the steps above.

Making Inferences

Simply put, an inference is making an educated guess drawn from evidence, logic, and reasoning. The key to making inferences is identifying clues within a passage, and then using common sense to arrive at a reasonable conclusion. Consider it "reading between the lines."

One way to make an inference is to look for main topics. When doing so, pay particular attention to any titles, headlines, or opening statements made by the author. Topic sentences or repetitive ideas can be clues in gleaning inferred ideas. For example, if a passage contains the phrase *DNA testing, while some consider it infallible, is an inherently flawed technique,* the test taker can infer the rest of the passage will contain information that points to DNA testing's infallibility.

The test taker may be asked to make an inference based on prior knowledge, but they may also be asked to make predictions based on new ideas. For example, the test taker may have no prior knowledge of DNA other than its genetic property to replicate. However, if the reader is given passages on the flaws of DNA testing with enough factual evidence, the test taker may arrive at the inferred conclusion that the author does not support the infallibility of DNA testing in all identification cases.

When making inferences, it is important to remember that the critical thinking process involved must be fluid and open to change. While a reader may infer an idea from a main topic, general statement, or other clues, they must be open to receiving new information within a particular passage. New ideas presented by an author may require the test taker to alter an inference. Similarly, when asked questions that require making an inference, it's important to read the entire test passage and all of the answer options. Often, a test taker will need to refine a general inference based on new ideas that may be presented within the test itself.

Author's Use of Evidence to Support Claims

Authors utilize a wide range of techniques to tell a story or communicate information. Readers should be familiar with the most common of these techniques. Techniques of writing are also commonly known as rhetorical devices, and they are some of the evidence that authors use to support claims.

In non-fiction writing, authors employ argumentative techniques to present their opinion to readers in the most convincing way. First of all, persuasive writing usually includes at least one type of appeal: an appeal to logic (logos), emotion (pathos), or credibility and trustworthiness (ethos). When a writer appeals to logic, they are asking readers to agree with them based on research, evidence, and an established line of reasoning. An author's argument might also appeal to readers' emotions, perhaps by including personal stories and anecdotes (a short narrative of a specific event). A final type of appeal, appeal to authority, asks the reader to agree with the author's argument on the basis of their expertise or credentials. Consider three different approaches to arguing the same opinion:

<u>Logic (Logos)</u>
Below is an example of an appeal to logic. The author uses evidence to disprove the logic of the school's rule (the rule was supposed to reduce discipline problems; the number of problems has not been reduced; therefore, the rule is not working) and call for its repeal.

> Our school should abolish its current ban on cell phone use on campus. This rule was adopted last year as an attempt to reduce class disruptions and help students focus more on their lessons. However, since the rule was enacted, there has been no change in the number of disciplinary problems in class. Therefore, the rule is ineffective and should be done away with.

<u>Emotion (Pathos)</u>
An author's argument might also appeal to readers' emotions, perhaps by including personal stories and anecdotes.

The next example presents an appeal to emotion. By sharing the personal anecdote of one student and speaking about emotional topics like family relationships, the author invokes the reader's empathy in asking them to reconsider the school rule.

> Our school should abolish its current ban on cell phone use on campus. If they aren't able to use their phones during the school day, many students feel isolated from their loved ones. For example, last semester, one student's grandmother had a heart attack in the morning. However, because he couldn't use his cell phone, the student didn't know about his grandmother's accident until the end of the day—when she had already passed away and it was too late to say goodbye. By preventing students from contacting their friends and family, our school is placing undue stress and anxiety on students.

<u>Credibility (Ethos)</u>
Finally, an appeal to authority includes a statement from a relevant expert. In this case, the author uses a doctor in the field of education to support the argument. All three examples begin from the same

opinion—the school's phone ban needs to change—but rely on different argumentative styles to persuade the reader.

> Our school should abolish its current ban on cell phone use on campus. According to Dr. Bartholomew Everett, a leading educational expert, "Research studies show that cell phone usage has no real impact on student attentiveness. Rather, phones provide a valuable technological resource for learning. Schools need to learn how to integrate this new technology into their curriculum." Rather than banning phones altogether, our school should follow the advice of experts and allow students to use phones as part of their learning.

Informational Graphics

A test taker's ability to draw conclusions from an informational graphic is a sub-skill in displaying one's command of reading evidence. Drawing conclusions requires the reader to consider all information provided in the passage, then to use logic to piece it together to form a reasonably correct resolution. In this case, a test taker must look for facts as well as opinionated statements. Both should be considered in order to arrive at a conclusion. These types of questions test one's ability to conduct logical and analytical thinking.

Identifying data-driven evidence in informational graphics is very similar to analyzing factual information. However, it often involves the use of graphics in order to do so. In these types of questions, the test taker will be presented with a graph, or organizational tool, and asked questions regarding the information it contains. On the following page, review the pie chart organizing percentages of primary occupations of public transportation passengers in US cities.

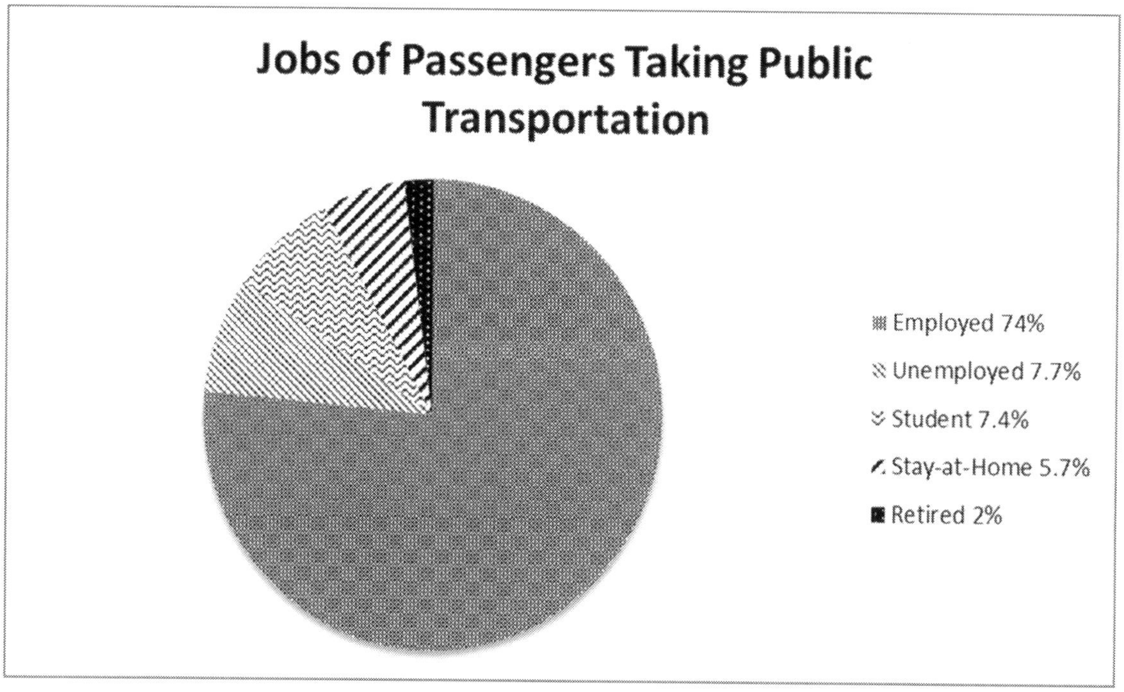

This figure depicts the jobs of passengers taking public transportation in U.S. cities. A corresponding SAT question may have the test taker study the chart, then answer a question regarding the values. For example, is the number of students relying on public transportation greater or less than the number of the unemployed? Similarly, the test may ask if people employed outside the home are less likely to use public transportation than homemakers. Note that the phrase *less likely* may weigh into the reader's choice of optional answers and that the test taker should look for additional passage data to arrive at a conclusion one way or another.

Words in Context

In order to successfully complete the Reading section of the SAT, the test taker should be able to identify words in context. This involves a set of skills that requires the test taker to answer questions about unfamiliar words within a particular text passage. Additionally, the test taker may be asked to answer critical thinking questions based on unfamiliar word meaning. Identifying words in context is very much like solving a puzzle. By using a variety of techniques, a test taker should be able to correctly identify unfamiliar words and concepts with ease.

Using Context Clues

A context clue is a hint that an author provides to the reader in order to help define difficult or unique words. When reading a passage, a test taker should take note of any unfamiliar words, and then examine the sentence around them to look for clues to the word meanings. Let's look at an example:

> He faced a *conundrum* in making this decision. He felt as if he had come to a crossroads. This was truly a puzzle, and what he did next would determine the course of his future.

The word *conundrum* may be unfamiliar to the reader. By looking at context clues, the reader should be able to determine its meaning. In this passage, context clues include the idea of making a decision and of being unsure. Furthermore, the author restates the definition of conundrum in using the word *puzzle* as a synonym. Therefore, the reader should be able to determine that the definition of the word *conundrum* is a difficult puzzle.

Similarly, a reader can determine difficult vocabulary by identifying antonyms. Let's look at an example:

> Her *gregarious* nature was completely opposite of her twin's, who was shy, retiring, and socially nervous.

The word *gregarious* may be unfamiliar. However, by looking at the surrounding context clues, the reader can determine that *gregarious* does not mean shy. The twins' personalities are being contrasted. Therefore, *gregarious* must mean sociable, or something similar to it.

At times, an author will provide contextual clues through a cause and effect relationship. Look at the next sentence as an example:

> The athletes were excited with *elation* when they won the tournament; unfortunately, their off-court antics caused them to forfeit the win.

The word *elation* may be unfamiliar to the reader. However, the author defines the word by presenting a cause and effect relationship. The athletes were so elated at the win that their behavior went overboard and they had to forfeit. In this instance, *elated* must mean something akin to overjoyed, happy, and overexcited.

Cause and effect is one technique authors use to demonstrate relationships. A cause is why something happens. The effect is what happens as a result. For example, a reader may encounter text such as

Because he was unable to sleep, he was often restless and irritable during the day. The cause is insomnia due to lack of sleep. The effect is being restless and irritable. When reading for a cause and effect relationship, look for words such as "if", "then", "such", and "because." By using cause and effect, an author can describe direct relationships, and convey an overall theme, particularly when taking a stance on their topic.

An author can also provide contextual clues through comparison and contrast. Let's look at an example:

> Her torpid state caused her parents, and her physician, to worry about her seemingly sluggish well-being.

The word *torpid* is probably unfamiliar to the reader. However, the author has compared *torpid* to a state of being and, moreover, one that's worrisome. Therefore, the reader should be able to determine that *torpid* is not a positive, healthy state of being. In fact, through the use of comparison, it means sluggish. Similarly, an author may contrast an unfamiliar word with an idea. In the sentence *Her <u>torpid</u> state was completely opposite of her usual, bubbly self,* the meaning of *torpid*, or sluggish, is contrasted with the words *bubbly self*.

A test taker should be able to critically assess and determine unfamiliar word meanings through the use of an author's context clues in order to fully comprehend difficult text passages.

<u>Relating Unfamiliar Words to Familiar Words</u>

The Reading section of the SAT will test a reader's ability to use context clues, and then relate unfamiliar words to more familiar ones. Using the word *torpid* as an example, the test may ask the test taker to relate the meaning of the word to a list of vocabulary options and choose the more familiar word as closest in meaning. In this case, the test may say something like the following:

> Which of the following words means the same as the word *torpid* in the above passage?

Then they will provide the test taker with a list of familiar options such as happy, disgruntled, sluggish, and animated. By using context clues, the reader has already determined the meaning of *torpid* as slow or sluggish, so the reader should be able to correctly identify the word *sluggish* as the correct answer.

One effective way to relate unfamiliar word meanings to more familiar ones is to substitute the provided word answer options with the unfamiliar word in question. Although this will not always lead to a correct answer every time, this strategy will help the test taker narrow answer options. Be careful when utilizing this strategy. Pay close attention to the meaning of sentences and answer choices because it's easy to mistake answer choices as correct when they are easily substituted, especially when they are the same part of speech. Does the sentence mean the same thing with the substituted word option in place or does it change entirely? Does the substituted word make sense? Does it possibly mean the same as the unfamiliar word in question?

How an Author's Word Choice Shapes Meaning, Style, and Tone

Authors choose their words carefully in order to artfully depict meaning, style, and tone, which is most commonly inferred through the use of adjectives and verbs. The *tone* is the predominant emotion present in the text and represents the attitude or feelings that an author has towards a character or event.

To review, an adjective is a word used to describe something, and usually precedes the noun, a person, place, or object. A verb is a word describing an action. For example, the sentence "The scary woodpecker ate the spider" includes the adjective "scary," the noun "woodpecker," and the verb "ate." Reading this sentence may rouse some negative feelings, as the word "scary" carries a negative charge. The *charge* is the emotional connotation that can be derived from the adjectives and verbs and is either positive or negative. Recognizing the charge of a particular sentence or passage is an effective way to understand the meaning and tone the author is trying to convey.

Many authors have conflicting charges within the same text, but a definitive tone can be inferred by understanding the meaning of the charges relative to each other. It's important to recognize key conjunctions, or words that link sentences or clauses together. There are several types and subtypes of conjunctions. Three are most important for reading comprehension:

- *Cumulative conjunctions* add one statement to another.
- Examples: and, both, also, as well as, not only
- I.e. The juice is sweet *and* sour.
- *Adversative conjunctions* are used to contrast two clauses.
- Examples: but, while, still, yet, nevertheless
- I.e. She was tired *but* she was happy.
- *Alternative conjunctions* express two alternatives.
- Examples: or, either, neither, nor, else, otherwise
- I.e. He must eat *or* he will die.

Identifying the meaning and tone of a text can be accomplished with the following techniques:

- Identify the adjectives and verbs.
- Recognize any important conjunctions.
- Label the adjectives and verbs as positive or negative.
- Understand what the charge means about the text.

To demonstrate these steps, examine the following passage from the classic children's poem, "The Sheep":

> Lazy sheep, pray tell me why
>
> In the pleasant fields you lie,
>
> Eating grass, and daisies white,
>
> From the morning till the night?
>
> Everything can something do,
>
> But what kind of use are you?

–Taylor, Jane and Ann. "The Sheep."

This selection is a good example of conflicting charges that work together to express an overall tone. Following the first two steps, identify the adjectives, verbs, and conjunctions within the passage. For this example, the adjectives are <u>underlined</u>, the verbs are in **bold**, and the conjunctions *italicized*:

> <u>Lazy</u> sheep, pray **tell** me why
>
> In the <u>pleasant</u> fields you **lie**,
>
> **Eating** grass, and daisies <u>white,</u>
>
> From the morning till the night?
>
> Everything can something do,
>
> *But* what kind of use are you?

For step three, read the passage and judge whether feelings of positivity or negativity arose. Then assign a charge to each of the words that were outlined. This can be done in a table format, or simply by writing a + or − next to the word.

The word <u>lazy</u> carries a negative connotation; it usually denotes somebody unwilling to work. To **tell** someone something has an exclusively neutral connotation, as it depends on what's being told, which has not yet been revealed at this point, so a charge can be assigned later. The word <u>pleasant</u> is an inherently positive word. To **lie** could be positive or negative depending on the context, but as the subject (the sheep) is lying in a pleasant field, then this is a positive experience. **Eating** is also generally positive.

After labeling the charges for each word, it might be inferred that the tone of this poem is happy and maybe even admiring or innocuously envious. However, notice the adversative conjunction, "but" and what follows. The author has listed all the pleasant things this sheep gets to do all day, but the tone changes when the author asks, "What kind of use are you?" Asking someone to prove their value is a rather hurtful thing to do, as it implies that the person asking the question doesn't believe the subject has any value, so this could be listed under negative charges. Referring back to the verb **tell**, after reading the whole passage, it can be deduced that the author is asking the sheep to tell what use the sheep is, so this has a negative charge.

+	−
• Pleasant • Lie in fields • From morning to night	• Lazy • Tell me • What kind of use are you

Upon examining the charges, it might seem like there's an even amount of positive and negative emotion in this selection, and that's where the conjunction "but" becomes crucial to identifying the tone. The conjunction "but" indicates there's a contrasting view to the pleasantness of the sheep's daily life, and this view is that the sheep is lazy and useless, which is also indicated by the first line, "lazy sheep, pray tell me why."

It might be helpful to look at questions pertaining to tone. For this selection, consider the following question:

The author of the poem regards the sheep with a feeling of what?

a. Respect
b. Disgust
c. Apprehension
d. Intrigue

Considering the author views the sheep as lazy with nothing to offer, Choice *A* appears to reflect the opposite of what the author is feeling.

Choice *B* seems to mirror the author's feelings towards the sheep, as laziness is considered a disreputable trait, and people (or personified animals, in this case) with unfavorable traits might be viewed with disgust.

Choice *C* doesn't make sense within context, as laziness isn't usually feared.

Choice *D* is tricky, as it may be tempting to argue that the author is intrigued with the sheep because they ask, "pray tell me why." This is another out-of-scope answer choice as it doesn't *quite* describe the feelings the author experiences and there's also a much better fit in Choice *B*.

Analysis in History/Social Studies and in Science

The Reading section of the SAT will include one passage from social sciences such as history, economics, psychology, or sociology. For these types of passages and questions, the test taker will need to utilize all their reading comprehension skills, but mastery of further skills will help. This section addresses those skills.

Comprehending Test Questions Prior to Reading

While preparing for a historical passage on a standardized test, first read the test questions, and then quickly scan the test answers prior to reading the passage itself. Notice there is a difference between the terms *read* and *scans*. Reading involves full concentration while addressing every word. Scanning involves quickly glancing at text in chunks, noting important dates, words, and ideas along the way. Reading test questions will help the test taker know what information to focus on in the historical passage. Scanning answers will help the test taker focus on possible answer options while reading the passage.

When reading standardized test questions that address historical passages, be sure to clearly understand what each question is asking. Is a question asking about vocabulary? Is another asking for the test taker to find a specific historical fact? Do any of the questions require the test taker to draw conclusions, identify an author's topic, tone, or position? Knowing what content to address will help the test taker focus on the information they will be asked about later. However, the test taker should approach this reading comprehension technique with some caution. It is tempting to only look for the right answers within any given passage. Do not put on "reading blinders" and ignore all other information presented in a passage. It is important to fully read every passage and not just scan it. Strictly looking for what may be the right answers to test questions can cause the test taker to ignore important contextual clues that actually require critical thinking in order to identify correct answers. Scanning a passage for what appears to be wrong answers can have a similar result.

When reading test questions prior to tackling a historical passage, be sure to understand what skills the test is assessing, and then fully read the related passage with those skills in mind. Focus on every word in both the test questions and the passage itself. Read with a critical eye and a logical mind.

Reading for Factual Information

Standardized test questions that ask for factual information are usually straightforward. These types of questions will either ask the test taker to confirm a fact by choosing a correct answer, or to select a correct answer based on a negative fact question.

For example, the test taker may encounter a passage from Lincoln's Gettysburg address. A corresponding test question may ask the following:

> Which war is Abraham Lincoln referring to in the following passage?: "Now we are engaged in a great civil war, testing whether that nation, or any nation so conceived and so dedicated, can long endure."

This type of question is asking the test taker to confirm a simple fact. Given options such as World War I, the War of Spanish Succession, World War II, and the American Civil War, the test taker should be able to correctly identify the American Civil War based on the words "civil war" within the passage itself, and, hopefully, through general knowledge. In this case, reading the test question and scanning answer options ahead of reading the Gettysburg address would help quickly identify the correct answer. Similarly, a test taker may be asked to confirm a historical fact based on a negative fact question. For example, a passage's corresponding test question may ask the following:

> Which option is incorrect based on the above passage?

Given a variety of choices speaking about which war Abraham Lincoln was addressing, the test taker would need to eliminate all correct answers pertaining to the American Civil War and choose the answer choice referencing a different war. In other words, the correct answer is the one that contradicts the information in the passage.

It is important to remember that reading for factual information is straightforward. The test taker must distinguish fact from bias. Factual statements can be proven or disproven independent of the author and from a variety of other sources. Remember, successfully answering questions regarding factual information may require the test taker to re-read the passage, as these types of questions test for attention to detail.

Reading for Tone, Message, and Effect

The SAT does not just address a test taker's ability to find facts within a historical reading passage; it also determines a reader's ability to determine an author's viewpoint through the use of tone, message, and overall effect. This type of reading comprehension requires inference skills, deductive reasoning skills, the ability to draw logical conclusions, and overall critical thinking skills. Reading for factual information is straightforward. Reading for an author's tone, message, and overall effect is not. It's key to read carefully when asked test questions that address a test taker's ability to these writing devices. These are not questions that can be easily answered by quickly scanning for the right information.

Tone

An author's *tone* is the use of particular words, phrases, and writing style to convey an overall meaning. Tone expresses the author's attitude towards a particular topic. For example, a historical reading passage may begin like the following:

> The presidential election of 1960 ushered in a new era, a new Camelot, a new phase of forward thinking in U.S. politics that embraced brash action, unrest, and responded with admirable leadership.

From this opening statement, a reader can draw some conclusions about the author's attitude towards President John F. Kennedy. Furthermore, the reader can make additional, educated guesses about the state of the Union during the 1960 presidential election. By close reading, the test taker can determine that the repeated use of the word *new* and words such as *admirable leadership* indicate the author's tone of admiration regarding the President's boldness. In addition, the author assesses that the era during President Kennedy's administration was problematic through the use of the words *brash action* and *unrest.* Therefore, if a test taker encountered a test question asking about the author's use of tone and their assessment of the Kennedy administration, the test taker should be able to identify an answer indicating admiration. Similarly, if asked about the state of the Union during the 1960s, a test taker should be able to correctly identify an answer indicating political unrest.

When identifying an author's tone, the following list of words may be helpful. This is not an inclusive list. Generally, parts of speech that indicate attitude will also indicate tone:

- Comical
- Angry
- Ambivalent
- Scary
- Lyrical
- Matter-of-fact
- Judgmental
- Sarcastic
- Malicious
- Objective
- Pessimistic
- Patronizing
- Gloomy
- Instructional
- Satirical
- Formal
- Casual

Message

An author's *message* is the same as the overall meaning of a passage. It is the main idea, or the main concept the author wishes to convey. An author's message may be stated outright or it may be implied. Regardless, the test taker will need to use careful reading skills to identify an author's message or purpose.

Often, the message of a particular passage can be determined by thinking about why the author wrote the information. Many historical passages are written to inform and to teach readers established, factual information. However, many historical works are also written to convey biased ideas to readers. Gleaning bias from an author's message in a historical passage can be difficult, especially if the reader is presented with a variety of established facts as well. Readers tend to accept historical writing as factual. This is not always the case. Any discerning reader who has tackled historical information on topics such as United States political party agendas can attest that two or more works on the same topic may have completely different messages supporting or refuting the value of the identical policies. Therefore, it is important to critically assess an author's message separate from factual information. One author, for example, may point to the rise of unorthodox political candidates in an election year based on the failures of the political party in office while another may point to the rise of the same candidates in the same election year based on the current party's successes. The historical facts of what has occurred leading up to an election year are not in refute. Labeling those facts as a failure or a success is a bias within an author's overall *message*, as is excluding factual information in order to further a particular point. In a standardized testing situation, a reader must be able to critically assess what the author is trying to say separate from the historical facts that surround their message.

Using the example of Lincoln's Gettysburg Address, a test question may ask the following:

> What is the message the author is trying to convey through this address?

Then they will ask the test taker to select an answer that best expresses Lincoln's *message* to his audience. Based on the options given, a test taker should be able to select the answer expressing the idea that Lincoln's audience should recognize the efforts of those who died in the war as a sacrifice to preserving human equality and self-government.

<u>Effect</u>

The *effect* an author wants to convey is when an author wants to impart a particular mood in their message. An author may want to challenge a reader's intellect, inspire imagination, or spur emotion. An author may present information to appeal to a physical, aesthetic, or transformational sense. Take the following text as an example:

> In 1963, Martin Luther King stated "I have a dream." The gathering at the Lincoln Memorial was the beginning of the Civil Rights movement and, with its reference to the Emancipation Proclamation, electrified those who wanted freedom and equality while rising from hatred and slavery. It was the beginning of radical change.

The test taker may be asked about the effect this statement might have on King's audience. Through careful reading of the passage, the test taker should be able to choose an answer that best identifies an effect of grabbing the audience's attention. The historical facts are in place: King made the speech in 1963 at the Lincoln Memorial, kicked off the civil rights movement, and referenced the Emancipation Proclamation. The words *electrified* and *radical change* indicate the effect the author wants the reader to understand as a result of King's speech. In this historical passage, facts are facts. However, the author's message goes above the facts to indicate the effect the message had on the audience and, in addition, the effect the event should have on the reader.

When reading historical passages, the test taker should perform due diligence in their awareness of the test questions and answers up front. From there, the test taker should carefully, and critically, read all historical excerpts with an eye for detail, tone, message (biased or unbiased), and effect. Being able to synthesize these skills will result in success in a standardized testing situation.

Science Passages

The SAT includes at least two science passages that address the fundamental concepts of Earth science, biology, chemistry, and/or physics. While prior general knowledge of these subjects is helpful in determining correct test answers, the test taker's ability to comprehend the passages is key to success. When reading scientific excerpts, the test taker must be able to examine quantitative information, identify hypotheses, interpret data, and consider implications of the material they are presented with. It is helpful, at this point, to reference the above section on comprehending test questions prior to reading. The same rules apply: read questions and scan questions, along with their answers, prior to fully reading a passage. Be informed prior to approaching a scientific text. A test taker should know what they will be asked and how to apply their reading skills. In this section of the test, it is also likely that a test taker will encounter graphs and charts to assess their ability to interpret scientific data with an appropriate conclusion. This section will determine the skills necessary to address scientific data presented through identifying hypotheses, through reading and examining data, and through interpreting data representation passages.

Examine Hypotheses

When presented with fundamental, scientific concepts, it is important to read for understanding. The most basic skill in achieving this literacy is to understand the concept of hypothesis and moreover, to be able to identify it in a particular passage. A hypothesis is a proposed idea that needs further investigation in order to be proven true or false. While it can be considered an educated guess, a hypothesis goes more in depth in its attempt to explain something that is not currently accepted within scientific theory. It requires further experimentation and data gathering to test its validity and is subject to change, based on scientifically conducted test results. Being able to read a science passage and understand its main purpose, including any hypotheses, helps the test taker understand data-driven evidence. It helps the test taker to be able to correctly answer questions about the science excerpt they are asked to read.

When reading to identify a hypothesis, a test taker should ask, "What is the passage trying to establish? What is the passage's main idea? What evidence does the passage contain that either supports or refutes this idea?" Asking oneself these questions will help identify a hypothesis. Additionally, hypotheses are logical statements that are testable, and use very precise language.

Review the following hypothesis example:

> Consuming excess sugar in the form of beverages has a greater impact on childhood obesity and subsequent weight gain than excessive sugar from food.

While this is likely a true statement, it is still only a conceptual idea in a text passage regarding sugar consumption in childhood obesity, unless the passage also contains tested data that either proves or disproves the statement. A test taker could expect the rest of the passage to cite data proving that children who drink empty calories and don't exercise will, in fact, be obese.

A hypothesis goes further in that, given its ability to be proven or disproven, it may result in further hypotheses that require extended research. For example, the hypothesis regarding sugar consumption in drinks, after undergoing rigorous testing, may lead scientists to state another hypothesis such as the following:

> Consuming excess sugar in the form of beverages as opposed to food items is a habit found in mostly sedentary children.

This new, working hypothesis further focuses not just on the source of an excess of calories, but tries an "educated guess" that empty caloric intake has a direct, subsequent impact on physical behavior.

The data-driven chart below is similar to an illustration a test taker might see in relation to the hypothesis on sugar consumption in children:

Behaviors of Healthy and Unhealthy Kids

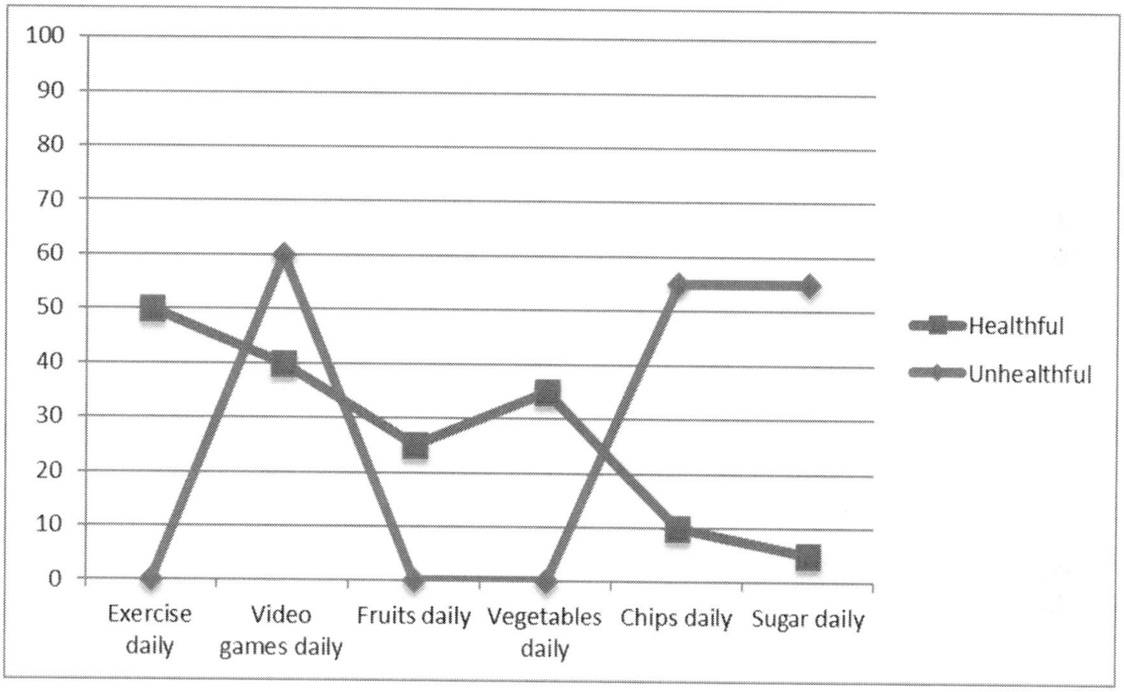

While this guide will address other data-driven passages a test taker could expect to see within a given science excerpt, note that the hypothesis regarding childhood sugar intake and rate of exercise has undergone scientific examination and yielded results that support its truth.

When reading a science passage to determine its hypothesis, a test taker should look for a concept that attempts to explain a phenomenon, is testable, logical, precisely worded, and yields data-driven results. The test taker should scan the presented passage for any word or data-driven clues that will help identify the hypothesis, and then be able to correctly answer test questions regarding the hypothesis based on their critical thinking skills.

Interpreting Data and Considering Implications

The Reading section of the SAT will contain one data-driven science passage that require the test taker to examine evidence within a particular type of graphic. The test taker will then be required to interpret the data and answer questions demonstrating their ability to draw logical conclusions.

In general, there are two types of data: qualitative and quantitative. Science passages may contain both, but simply put, quantitative data is reflected numerically and qualitative is not. Qualitative data is based on its qualities. In other words, qualitative data tends to present information more in subjective generalities (for example, relating to size or appearance). Quantitative data is based on numerical findings such as percentages. Quantitative data will be described in numerical terms. While both types of data are valid, the test taker will more likely be faced with having to interpret quantitative data through one or more graphic(s), and then be required to answer questions regarding the numerical data. The section of this study guide briefly addresses how data may be displayed in line graphs, bar charts, circle graphs, and scatter plots. A test taker should take the time to learn the skills it takes to interpret quantitative data. An example of a line graph is as follows:

Cell Phone Use in Kiteville, 2000-2006

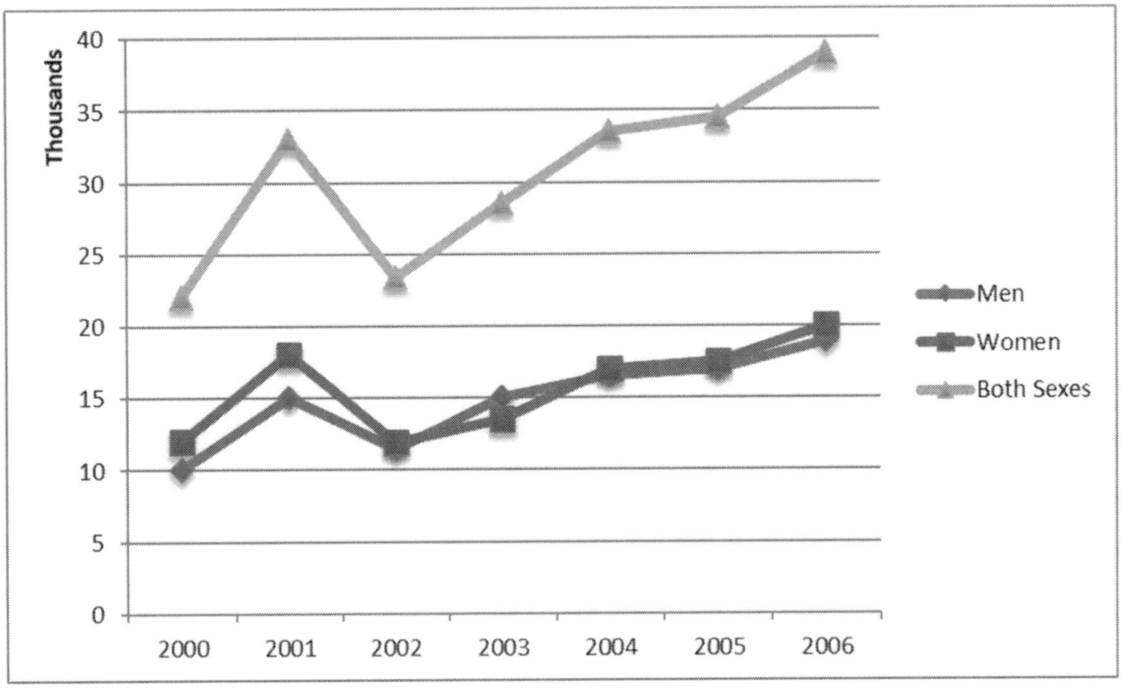

A line graph presents quantitative data on both horizontal (side to side) and vertical (up and down) axes. It requires the test taker to examine information across varying data points. When reading a line graph, a test taker should pay attention to any headings, as these indicate a title for the data it contains. In the above example, the test taker can anticipate the line graph contains numerical data regarding the use of cellphones during a certain time period. From there, a test taker should carefully read any outlying words or phrases that will help determine the meaning of data within the horizontal and vertical axes. In this example, the vertical axis displays the total number of people in increments of 5,000. Horizontally, the graph displays yearly markers, and the reader can assume the data presented accounts for a full calendar year. In addition, the line graph also defines its data points by shapes. Some data points represent the number of men. Some data points represent the number of women, and a third type of data point represents the number of both sexes combined.

A test taker may be asked to read and interpret the graph's data, then answer questions about it. For example, the test may ask, *In which year did men seem to decrease cellphone use?* then require the test taker to select the correct answer. Similarly, the test taker may encounter a question such as *Which year yielded the highest number of cellphone users overall?* The test taker should be able to identify the correct answer as 2006.

A bar graph presents quantitative data through the use of lines or rectangles. The height and length of these lines or rectangles corresponds to contain numerical data. The data presented may represent information over time, showing shaded data over time or over other defined parameters. A bar graph will also utilize horizontal and vertical axes. An example of a bar graph is as follows:

Population Growth in Major U.S. Cities

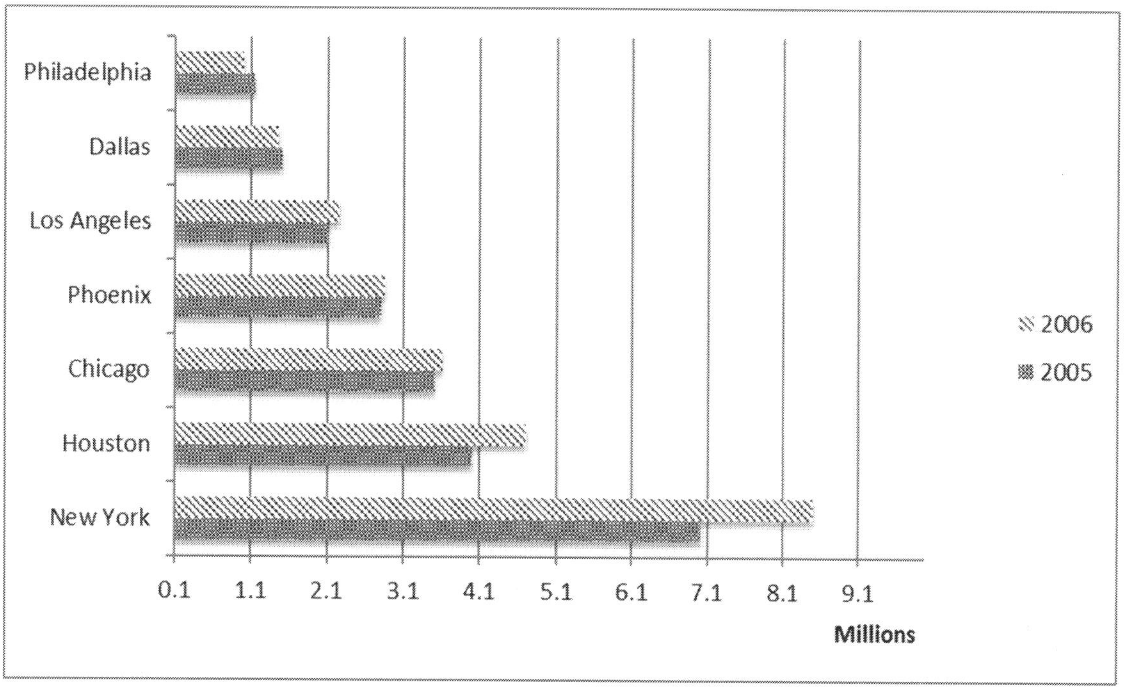

Reading the data in a bar graph is similar to the skills needed to read a line graph. The test taker should read and comprehend all heading information, as well as information provided along the horizontal and vertical axes. Note that the graph pertains to the population of some major U.S. cities. The "values" of these cities can be found along the left side of the graph, along the vertical axis. The population values can be found along the horizontal axes. Notice how the graph uses shaded bars to depict the change in population over time, as the heading indicates. Therefore, when the test taker is asked a question such as, *Which major U.S. city experienced the greatest amount of population growth during the depicted two-year cycle,* the reader should be able to determine a correct answer of New York. It is important to pay particular attention to color, length, data points, and both axes, as well as any outlying header information in order to be able to answer graph-like test questions.

A circle graph presents quantitative data in the form of a circle (also sometimes referred to as a pie chart). The same principles apply: the test taker should look for numerical data within the confines of the circle itself but also note any outlying information that may be included in a header, footer, or to the side of the circle. A circle graph will not depict horizontal or vertical axis information, but it will instead rely on the reader's ability to visually take note of segmented circle pieces and apply information accordingly. An example of a circle graph is as follows:

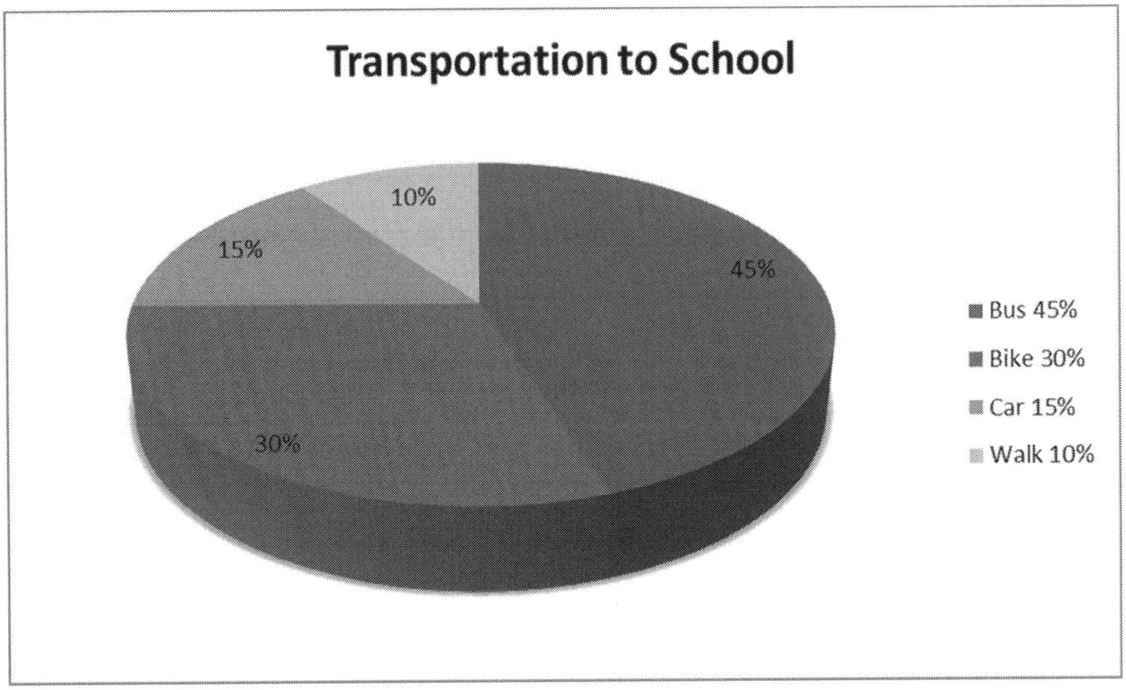

Notice the heading "Transportation to School." This should indicate to the test taker that the topic of the circle graph is how people traditionally get to school. To the right of the graph, the reader should comprehend that the data percentages contained within it directly correspond to the method of transportation. In this graph, the data is represented through the use shades and pattern. Each transportation method has its own shade. For example, if the test taker was then asked, *Which method of school transportation is most widely utilized,* the reader should be able to identify school bus as the correct answer.

Be wary of test questions that ask test takers to draw conclusions based on information that is not present. For example, it is not possible to determine, given the parameters of this circle graph, whether the population presented is of a particular gender or ethnic group. This graph does not represent data from a particular city or school district. It does not distinguish between student grade levels and, although the reader could infer that the typical student must be of driving age if cars are included, this is not necessarily the case. Elementary school students may rely on parents or others to drive them by personal methods. Therefore, do not read too much into data that is not presented. Only rely on the quantitative data that is presented in order to answer questions.

A scatter plot or scatter diagram is a graph that depicts quantitative data across plotted points. It will involve at least two sets of data. It will also involve horizontal and vertical axes.

An example of a scatter plot is as follows:

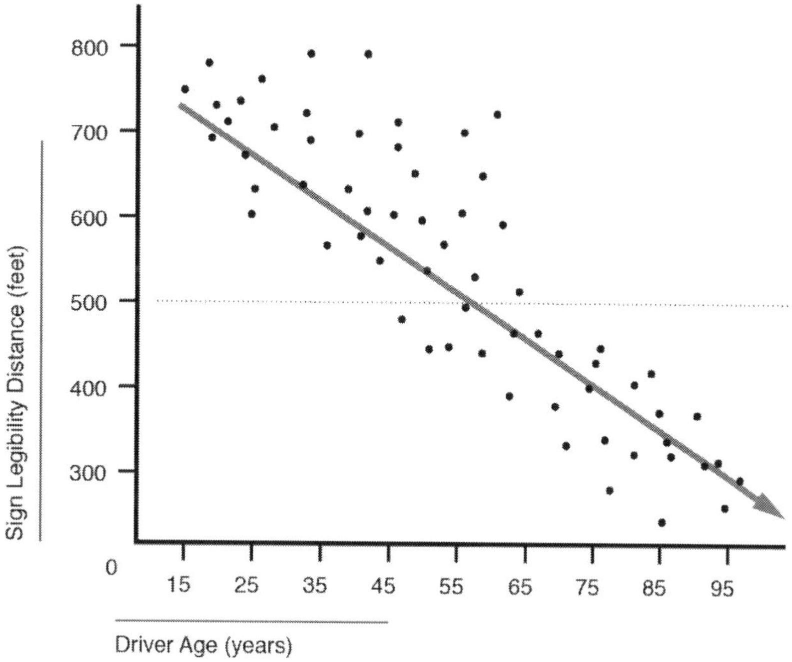

The skills needed to address a scatter plot are essentially the same as in other graph examples. Note any topic headings, as well as horizontal or vertical axis information. In the sample above, the reader can determine the data addresses a driver's ability to correctly and legibly read road signs as related to their age. Again, note the information that is absent. The test taker is not given the data to assess a time period, location, or driver gender. It simply requires the reader to note an approximate age to the ability to correctly identify road signs from a distance measured in feet. Notice that the overall graph also displays a trend. In this case, the data indicates a negative one and possibly supports the hypothesis that as a driver ages, their ability to correctly read a road sign at over 500 feet tends to decline over time. If the test taker were to be asked, *At what approximation in feet does a sixteen-year-old driver correctly see and read a street sign,* the answer would be the option closest to 500 feet.

Reading and examining scientific data in excerpts involves all of a reader's contextual reading, data interpretation, drawing logical conclusions based only on the information presented, and their application of critical thinking skills across a set of interpretive questions. Thorough comprehension and attention to detail is necessary to achieve test success.

Practice Questions

Passage #1

Questions 1–6 are based upon the following passage:

This excerpt is an adaptation of Jonathan Swift's *Gulliver's Travels into Several Remote Nations of the World.*

> My gentleness and good behaviour had gained so far on the emperor and his court, and indeed upon the army and people in general, that I began to conceive hopes of getting my liberty in a short time. I took all possible methods to cultivate this favourable disposition. The natives came, by degrees, to be less apprehensive of any danger from me. I would sometimes lie down, and let five or six of them dance on my hand; and at last the boys and girls would venture to come and play at hide-and-seek in my hair. I had now made a good progress in understanding and speaking the language. The emperor had a mind one day to entertain me with several of the country shows, wherein they exceed all nations I have known, both for dexterity and magnificence. I was diverted with none so much as that of the rope-dancers, performed upon a slender white thread, extended about two feet, and twelve inches from the ground. Upon which I shall desire liberty, with the reader's patience, to enlarge a little.
>
> This diversion is only practised by those persons who are candidates for great employments, and high favour at court. They are trained in this art from their youth, and are not always of noble birth, or liberal education. When a great office is vacant, either by death or disgrace (which often happens,) five or six of those candidates petition the emperor to entertain his majesty and the court with a dance on the rope; and whoever jumps the highest, without falling, succeeds in the office. Very often the chief ministers themselves are commanded to show their skill, and to convince the emperor that they have not lost their faculty. Flimnap, the treasurer, is allowed to cut a caper on the straight rope, at least an inch higher than any other lord in the whole empire. I have seen him do the summerset several times together, upon a trencher fixed on a rope which is no thicker than a common packthread in England. My friend Reldresal, principal secretary for private affairs, is, in my opinion, if I am not partial, the second after the treasurer; the rest of the great officers are much upon a par.

1. Which of the following statements best summarize the central purpose of this text?
    a. Gulliver details his fondness for the archaic yet interesting practices of his captors.
    b. Gulliver conjectures about the intentions of the aristocratic sector of society.
    c. Gulliver becomes acquainted with the people and practices of his new surroundings.
    d. Gulliver's differences cause him to become penitent around new acquaintances.

2. What is the word *principal* referring to in the following text?

My friend Reldresal, principal secretary for private affairs, is, in my opinion, if I am not partial, the second after the treasurer; the rest of the great officers are much upon a par.

a. Primary or chief
b. An acolyte
c. An individual who provides nurturing
d. One in a subordinate position

3. What can the reader infer from this passage?

I would sometimes lie down, and let five or six of them dance on my hand; and at last the boys and girls would venture to come and play at hide-and-seek in my hair.

a. The children tortured Gulliver.
b. Gulliver traveled because he wanted to meet new people.
c. Gulliver is considerably larger than the children who are playing around him.
d. Gulliver has a genuine love and enthusiasm for people of all sizes.

4. What is the significance of the word *mind* in the following passage?

The emperor had a mind one day to entertain me with several of the country shows, wherein they exceed all nations I have known, both for dexterity and magnificence.

a. The ability to think
b. A collective vote
c. A definitive decision
d. A mythological question

5. Which of the following assertions does not support the fact that games are a commonplace event in this culture?

a. My gentlest and good behavior . . . short time.
b. They are trained in this art from their youth . . . liberal education.
c. Very often the chief ministers themselves are commanded to show their skill . . . not lost their faculty.
d. Flimnap, the treasurer, is allowed to cut a caper on the straight rope . . . higher than any other lord in the whole empire.

6. How do the roles of Flimnap and Reldresal serve as evidence of the community's emphasis in regards to the correlation between physical strength and leadership abilities?

a. Only children used Gulliver's hands as a playground.
b. The two men who exhibited superior abilities held prominent positions in the community.
c. Only common townspeople, not leaders, walk the straight rope.
d. No one could jump higher than Gulliver.

Passage #2

Questions 7–12 are based upon the following passage:

This excerpt is adaptation of Robert Louis Stevenson's *The Strange Case of Dr. Jekyll and Mr. Hyde.*

"Did you ever come across a protégé of his—one Hyde?" He asked.

"Hyde?" repeated Lanyon. "No. Never heard of him. Since my time."

That was the amount of information that the lawyer carried back with him to the great, dark bed on which he tossed to and fro until the small hours of the morning began to grow large. It was a night of little ease to his toiling mind, toiling in mere darkness and besieged by questions.

Six o'clock struck on the bells of the church that was so conveniently near to Mr. Utterson's dwelling, and still he was digging at the problem. Hitherto it had touched him on the intellectual side alone; but; but now his imagination also was engaged, or rather enslaved; and as he lay and tossed in the gross darkness of the night in the curtained room, Mr. Enfield's tale went by before his mind in a scroll of lighted pictures. He would be aware of the great field of lamps in a nocturnal city; then of the figure of a man walking swiftly; then of a child running from the doctor's; and then these met, and that human Juggernaut trod the child down and passed on regardless of her screams. Or else he would see a room in a rich house, where his friend lay asleep, dreaming and smiling at his dreams; and then the door of that room would be opened, the curtains of the bed plucked apart, the sleeper recalled, and, lo! There would stand by his side a figure to whom power was given, and even at that dead hour he must rise and do its bidding. The figure in these two phrases haunted the lawyer all night; and if at anytime he dozed over, it was but to see it glide more stealthily through sleeping houses, or move the more swiftly, and still the more smoothly, even to dizziness, through wider labyrinths of lamplighted city, and at every street corner crush a child and leave her screaming. And still the figure had no face by which he might know it; even in his dreams it had no face, or one that baffled him and melted before his eyes; and thus there it was that there sprung up and grew apace in the lawyer's mind a singularly strong, almost an inordinate, curiosity to behold the features of the real Mr. Hyde. If he could but once set eyes on him, he thought the mystery would lighten and perhaps roll altogether away, as was the habit of mysterious things when well examined. He might see a reason for his friend's strange preference or bondage, and even for the startling clauses of the will. And at least it would be a face worth seeing: the face of a man who was without bowels of mercy: a face which had but to show itself to raise up, in the mind of the unimpressionable Enfield, a spirit of enduring hatred.

From that time forward, Mr. Utterson began to haunt the door in the by street of shops. In the morning before office hours, at noon when business was plenty of time scarce, at night under the face of the full city moon, by all lights and at all hours of solitude or concourse, the lawyer was to be found on his chosen post.

"If he be Mr. Hyde," he had thought, "I should be Mr. Seek."

7. What is the purpose of the use of repetition in the following passage?

> It was a night of little ease to his toiling mind, toiling in mere darkness and besieged by questions.

a. It serves as a demonstration of the mental state of Mr. Lanyon.
b. It is reminiscent of the church bells that are mentioned in the story.
c. It mimics Mr. Utterson's ambivalence.
d. It emphasizes Mr. Utterson's anguish in failing to identify Hyde's whereabouts.

8. What is the setting of the story in this passage?

a. In the city
b. On the countryside
c. In a jail
d. In a mental health facility

9. What can one infer about the meaning of the word "Juggernaut" from the author's use of it in the passage?

a. It is an apparition that appears at daybreak.
b. It scares children.
c. It is associated with space travel.
d. Mr. Utterson finds it soothing.

10. What is the definition of the word *haunt* in the following passage?

> From that time forward, Mr. Utterson began to haunt the door in the by street of shops. In the morning before office hours, at noon when business was plenty of time scarce, at night under the face of the full city moon, by all lights and at all hours of solitude or concourse, the lawyer was to be found on his chosen post.

a. To levitate
b. To constantly visit
c. To terrorize
d. To daunt

11. The phrase *labyrinths of lamplighted city* contains an example of what?

a. Hyperbole
b. Simile
c. Metaphor
d. Alliteration

12. What can one reasonably conclude from the final comment of this passage?

> "If he be Mr. Hyde," he had thought, "I should be Mr. Seek."

a. The speaker is considering a name change.
b. The speaker is experiencing an identity crisis.
c. The speaker has mistakenly been looking for the wrong person.
d. The speaker intends to continue to look for Hyde.

Passage #3

Questions 13–18 are based upon the following passage:

This excerpt is adaptation from "What to the Slave is the Fourth of July?" Rochester, New York July 5, 1852

Fellow citizens—Pardon me, and allow me to ask, why am I called upon to speak here today? What have I, or those I represent, to do with your national independence? Are the great principles of political freedom and of natural justice embodied in that Declaration of Independence, Independence extended to us? And am I therefore called upon to bring our humble offering to the national altar, and to confess the benefits, and express devout gratitude for the blessings, resulting from your independence to us?

Would to God, both for your sakes and ours, ours that an affirmative answer could be truthfully returned to these questions! Then would my task be light, and my burden easy and delightful. For who is there so cold that a nation's sympathy could not warm him? Who so obdurate and dead to the claims of gratitude that would not thankfully acknowledge such priceless benefits? Who so stolid and selfish, that would not give his voice to swell the hallelujahs of a nation's jubilee, when the chains of servitude had been torn from his limbs? I am not that man. In a case like that, the dumb may eloquently speak, and the lame man leap as an hart.

But, such is not the state of the case. I say it with a sad sense of the disparity between us. I am not included within the pale of this glorious anniversary. Oh pity! Your high independence only reveals the immeasurable distance between us. The blessings in which you this day rejoice, I do not enjoy in common. The rich inheritance of justice, liberty, prosperity, and independence, bequeathed by your fathers, is shared by *you*, not by *me*. This Fourth of July is *yours,* not *mine*. You may rejoice, *I* must mourn. To drag a man in fetters into the grand illuminated temple of liberty, and call upon him to join you in joyous anthems, were inhuman mockery and sacrilegious irony. Do you mean, citizens, to mock me, by asking me to speak today? If so there is a parallel to your conduct. And let me warn you that it is dangerous to copy the example of a nation whose crimes, towering up to heaven, were thrown down by the breath of the Almighty, burying that nation and irrecoverable ruin! I can today take up the plaintive lament of a peeled and woe-smitten people.

By the rivers of Babylon, there we sat down. Yea! We wept when we remembered Zion. We hanged our harps upon the willows in the midst thereof. For there, they that carried us away captive, required of us a song; and they who wasted us required of us mirth, saying, "Sing us one of the songs of Zion." How can we sing the Lord's song in a strange land? If I forget thee, O Jerusalem, let my right hand forget her cunning. If I do not remember thee, let my tongue cleave to the roof of my mouth.

13. What is the tone of the first paragraph of this passage?
    a. Exasperated
    b. Inclusive
    c. Contemplative
    d. Nonchalant

14. Which word CANNOT be used synonymously with the term *obdurate* as it is conveyed in the text below?

> Who so obdurate and dead to the claims of gratitude, that would not thankfully acknowledge such priceless benefits?

a. Steadfast
b. Stubborn
c. Contented
d. Unwavering

15. What is the central purpose of this text?
a. To demonstrate the author's extensive knowledge of the Bible
b. To address the feelings of exclusion expressed by African Americans after the establishment of the Fourth of July holiday
c. To convince wealthy landowners to adopt new holiday rituals
d. To explain why minorities often relished the notion of segregation in government institutions

16. Which statement serves as evidence of the question above?
a. By the rivers of Babylon . . . down.
b. Fellow citizens . . . today.
c. I can . . . woe-smitten people.
d. The rich inheritance of justice . . . *not by me*.

17. The statement below features an example of which of the following literary devices?

> Oh pity! Your high independence only reveals the immeasurable distance between us.

a. Assonance
b. Parallelism
c. Amplification
d. Hyperbole

18. The speaker's use of biblical references, such as "rivers of Babylon" and the "songs of Zion," helps the reader to do all of the following EXCEPT:
a. Identify with the speaker through the use of common text.
b. Convince the audience that injustices have been committed by referencing another group of people who have been previously affected by slavery.
c. Display the equivocation of the speaker and those that he represents.
d. Appeal to the listener's sense of humanity.

Passage #4

Questions 19–24 are based upon the following passage:

This excerpt is an adaptation from Abraham Lincoln's Address Delivered at the Dedication of the Cemetery at Gettysburg, November 19, 1863.

> Four score and seven years ago our fathers brought forth on this continent, a new nation, conceived in liberty, and dedicated to the proposition that all men are created equal.

Now we are engaged in a great civil war, testing whether that nation, or any nation so conceived and so dedicated, can long endure. We are met on a great battlefield of that war. We have come to dedicate a portion of that field, as a final resting place for those who here gave their lives that this nation might live. It is altogether fitting and proper that we should do this.

But, in a larger sense, we cannot dedicate—we cannot consecrate that we cannot hallow—this ground. The brave men, living and dead, who struggled here, have consecrated it, far above our poor power to add or detract. The world will little note, nor long remember what we say here, but it can never forget what they did here. It is for us the living, rather, to be dedicated here to the unfinished work which they who fought here have thus far so nobly advanced. It is rather for us to be here and dedicated to the great task remaining before us—that from these honored dead we take increased devotion to that cause for which they gave the last full measure of devotion—that we here highly resolve that these dead shall not have died in vain—that these this nation, under God, shall have a new birth of freedom—and that government of people, by the people, for the people, shall not perish from the earth.

19. The best description for the phrase *four score and seven years ago* is which of the following?
    a. A unit of measurement
    b. A period of time
    c. A literary movement
    d. A statement of political reform

20. What is the setting of this text?
    a. A battleship off of the coast of France
    b. A desert plain on the Sahara Desert
    c. A battlefield in North America
    d. The residence of Abraham Lincoln

21. Which war is Abraham Lincoln referring to in the following passage?

    Now we are engaged in a great civil war, testing whether that nation, or any nation so conceived and so dedicated, can long endure.

    a. World War I
    b. The War of the Spanish Succession
    c. World War II
    d. The American Civil War

22. What message is the author trying to convey through this address?
    a. The audience should consider the death of the people that fought in the war as an example and perpetuate the ideals of freedom that the soldiers died fighting for.
    b. The audience should honor the dead by establishing an annual memorial service.
    c. The audience should form a militia that would overturn the current political structure.
    d. The audience should forget the lives that were lost and discredit the soldiers.

23. Which rhetorical device is being used in the following passage?

> . . . we here highly resolve that these dead shall not have died in vain—that these this nation, under God, shall have a new birth of freedom—and that government of people, by the people, for the people, shall not perish from the earth.

a. Antimetabole
b. Antiphrasis
c. Anaphora
d. Epiphora

24. What is the effect of Lincoln's statement in the following passage?

> But, in a larger sense, we cannot dedicate—we cannot consecrate that we cannot hallow—this ground. The brave men, living and dead, who struggled here, have consecrated it, far above our poor power to add or detract.

a. His comparison emphasizes the great sacrifice of the soldiers who fought in the war.
b. His comparison serves as a remainder of the inadequacies of his audience.
c. His comparison serves as a catalyst for guilt and shame among audience members.
d. His comparison attempts to illuminate the great differences between soldiers and civilians.

Passage #5

Questions 25–30 are based upon the following passage:

This excerpt is adaptation from Charles Dickens' speech in Birmingham in England on December 30, 1853 on behalf of the Birmingham and Midland Institute.

> My Good Friends,—When I first imparted to the committee of the projected Institute my particular wish that on one of the evenings of my readings here the main body of my audience should be composed of working men and their families, I was animated by two desires; first, by the wish to have the great pleasure of meeting you face to face at this Christmas time, and accompany you myself through one of my little Christmas books; and second, by the wish to have an opportunity of stating publicly in your presence, and in the presence of the committee, my earnest hope that the Institute will, from the beginning, recognise one great principle—strong in reason and justice—which I believe to be essential to the very life of such an Institution. It is, that the working man shall, from the first unto the last, have a share in the management of an Institution which is designed for his benefit, and which calls itself by his name.
>
> I have no fear here of being misunderstood—of being supposed to mean too much in this. If there ever was a time when any one class could of itself do much for its own good, and for the welfare of society—which I greatly doubt—that time is unquestionably past. It is in the fusion of different classes, without confusion; in the bringing together of employers and employed; in the creating of a better common understanding among those whose interests are identical, who depend upon each other, who are vitally essential to each other, and who never can be in unnatural antagonism without deplorable results, that one of the chief principles of a Mechanics' Institution should consist. In this world a great deal of the bitterness among us arises from an imperfect understanding of one another. Erect in Birmingham a great Educational Institution, properly educational; educational of the feelings as well as of

the reason; to which all orders of Birmingham men contribute; in which all orders of Birmingham men meet; wherein all orders of Birmingham men are faithfully represented—and you will erect a Temple of Concord here which will be a model edifice to the whole of England.

Contemplating as I do the existence of the Artisans' Committee, which not long ago considered the establishment of the Institute so sensibly, and supported it so heartily, I earnestly entreat the gentlemen—earnest I know in the good work, and who are now among us,—by all means to avoid the great shortcoming of similar institutions; and in asking the working man for his confidence, to set him the great example and give him theirs in return. You will judge for yourselves if I promise too much for the working man, when I say that he will stand by such an enterprise with the utmost of his patience, his perseverance, sense, and support; that I am sure he will need no charitable aid or condescending patronage; but will readily and cheerfully pay for the advantages which it confers; that he will prepare himself in individual cases where he feels that the adverse circumstances around him have rendered it necessary; in a word, that he will feel his responsibility like an honest man, and will most honestly and manfully discharge it. I now proceed to the pleasant task to which I assure you I have looked forward for a long time.

25. Which word is most closely synonymous with the word *patronage* as it appears in the following statement?

> . . . that I am sure he will need no charitable aid or condescending patronage

a. Auspices
b. Aberration
c . Acerbic
d. Adulation

26. Which term is most closely aligned with the definition of the term *working man* as it is defined in the following passage?

> You will judge for yourselves if I promise too much for the working man, when I say that he will stand by such an enterprise with the utmost of his patience, his perseverance, sense, and support . . .

a. Plebian
b. Viscount
c. Entrepreneur
d. Bourgeois

27. Which of the following statements most closely correlates with the definition of the term *working man* as it is defined in Question 26?

a. A working man is not someone who works for institutions or corporations, but someone who is well versed in the workings of the soul.
b. A working man is someone who is probably not involved in social activities because the physical demand for work is too high.
c. A working man is someone who works for wages among the middle class.
d. The working man has historically taken to the field, to the factory, and now to the screen.

28. Based upon the contextual evidence provided in the passage above, what is the meaning of the term *enterprise* in the third paragraph?

a. Company
b. Courage
c. Game
d. Cause

29. The speaker addresses his audience as *My Good Friends*—what kind of credibility does this salutation give to the speaker?

a. The speaker is an employer addressing his employees, so the salutation is a way for the boss to bridge the gap between himself and his employees.
b. The speaker's salutation is one from an entertainer to his audience and uses the friendly language to connect to his audience before a serious speech.
c. The salutation gives the serious speech that follows a somber tone, as it is used ironically.
d. The speech is one from a politician to the public, so the salutation is used to grab the audience's attention.

30. According to the aforementioned passage, what is the speaker's second desire for his time in front of the audience?

a. To read a Christmas story
b. For the working man to have a say in his institution which is designed for his benefit.
c. To have an opportunity to stand in their presence
d. For the life of the institution to be essential to the audience as a whole

Passage #6

Questions 31–36 are based upon the following passage:

This excerpt is adapted from *Our Vanishing Wildlife,* by William T. Hornaday

> Three years ago, I think there were not many bird-lovers in the United States, who believed it possible to prevent the total extinction of both egrets from our fauna. All the known rookeries accessible to plume-hunters had been totally destroyed. Two years ago, the secret discovery of several small, hidden colonies prompted William Dutcher, President of the National Association of Audubon Societies, and Mr. T. Gilbert Pearson, Secretary, to attempt the protection of those colonies. With a fund contributed for the purpose, wardens were hired and duly commissioned. As previously stated, one of those wardens was shot dead in cold blood by a plume hunter. The task of guarding swamp rookeries from the attacks of money-hungry desperadoes to whom the accursed plumes were worth their weight in gold, is a very chancy proceeding. There is now one warden in Florida who says that "before they get my rookery they will first have to get me."
>
> Thus far the protective work of the Audubon Association has been successful. Now there are twenty colonies, which contain all told, about 5,000 egrets and about 120,000 herons and ibises which are guarded by the Audubon wardens. One of the most important is on Bird Island, a mile out in Orange Lake, central Florida, and it is ably defended by Oscar E. Baynard. To-day, the plume hunters who do not dare to raid the guarded rookeries are trying to study out the lines of flight of the birds, to and from their feeding-grounds, and shoot them in transit. Their motto is—"Anything to beat the law, and get the plumes." It is there that the state of Florida should take part in the war.

The success of this campaign is attested by the fact that last year a number of egrets were seen in eastern Massachusetts—for the first time in many years. And so to-day the question is, can the wardens continue to hold the plume-hunters at bay?

31. The author's use of first person pronoun in the following text does NOT have which of the following effects?

Three years ago, I think there were not many bird-lovers in the United States, who believed it possible to prevent the total extinction of both egrets from our fauna.

a. The phrase *I think* acts as a sort of hedging, where the author's tone is less direct and/or absolute.
b. It allows the reader to more easily connect with the author.
c. It encourages the reader to empathize with the egrets.
d. It distances the reader from the text by overemphasizing the story.

32. What purpose does the quote serve at the end of the first paragraph?
a. The quote shows proof of a hunter threatening one of the wardens.
b. The quote lightens the mood by illustrating the colloquial language of the region.
c. The quote provides an example of a warden protecting one of the colonies.
d. The quote provides much needed comic relief in the form of a joke.

33. What is the meaning of the word *rookeries* in the following text?

To-day, the plume hunters who do not dare to raid the guarded rookeries are trying to study out the lines of flight of the birds, to and from their feeding-grounds, and shoot them in transit.

a. Houses in a slum area
b. A place where hunters gather to trade tools
c. A place where wardens go to trade stories
d. A colony of breeding birds

34. What is on Bird Island?
a. Hunters selling plumes
b. An important bird colony
c. Bird Island Battle between the hunters and the wardens
d. An important egret with unique plumes

35. What is the main purpose of the passage?
a. To persuade the audience to act in preservation of the bird colonies
b. To show the effect hunting egrets has had on the environment
c. To argue that the preservation of bird colonies has had a negative impact on the environment.
d. To demonstrate the success of the protective work of the Audubon Association

36. Why are hunters trying to study the lines of flight of the birds?
a. To study ornithology, one must know the lines of flight that birds take.
b. To help wardens preserve the lives of the birds
c. To have a better opportunity to hunt the birds
d. To builds their homes under the lines of flight because they believe it brings good luck

Passage #8

Objective: Read and comprehend an excerpt written from a scientific perspective.

Questions 37–42 are based upon the following passage:

This excerpt is adaptation from *The Life-Story of Insects,* by Geo H. Carpenter.

> Insects as a whole are preeminently creatures of the land and the air. This is shown not only by the possession of wings by a vast majority of the class, but by the mode of breathing to which reference has already been made, a system of branching air-tubes carrying atmospheric air with its combustion-supporting oxygen to all the insect's tissues. The air gains access to these tubes through a number of paired air-holes or spiracles, arranged segmentally in series.
>
> It is of great interest to find that, nevertheless, a number of insects spend much of their time under water. This is true of not a few in the perfect winged state, as for example aquatic beetles and water-bugs ('boatmen' and 'scorpions') which have some way of protecting their spiracles when submerged, and, possessing usually the power of flight, can pass on occasion from pond or stream to upper air. But it is advisable in connection with our present subject to dwell especially on some insects that remain continually under water till they are ready to undergo their final moult and attain the winged state, which they pass entirely in the air. The preparatory instars of such insects are aquatic; the adult instar is aerial. All may-flies, dragon-flies, and caddis-flies, many beetles and two-winged flies, and a few moths thus divide their life-story between the water and the air. For the present we confine attention to the Stone-flies, the May-flies, and the Dragon-flies, three well-known orders of insects respectively called by systematists the Plecoptera, the Ephemeroptera and the Odonata.
>
> In the case of many insects that have aquatic larvae, the latter are provided with some arrangement for enabling them to reach atmospheric air through the surface-film of the water. But the larva of a stone-fly, a dragon-fly, or a may-fly is adapted more completely than these for aquatic life; it can, by means of gills of some kind, breathe the air dissolved in water.

37. Which statement best details the central idea in this passage?
    a. It introduces certain insects that transition from water to air.
    b. It delves into entomology, especially where gills are concerned.
    c. It defines what constitutes as insects' breathing.
    d. It invites readers to have a hand in the preservation of insects.

38. Which definition most closely relates to the usage of the word *moult* in the passage?
    a. An adventure of sorts, especially underwater
    b. Mating act between two insects
    c. The act of shedding part or all of the outer shell
    d. Death of an organism that ends in a revival of life

39. What is the purpose of the first paragraph in relation to the second paragraph?

a. The first paragraph serves as a cause and the second paragraph serves as an effect.

b. The first paragraph serves as a contrast to the second.

c. The first paragraph is a description for the argument in the second paragraph.

d. The first and second paragraphs are merely presented in a sequence.

40. What does the following sentence most nearly mean?

The preparatory instars of such insects are aquatic; the adult instar is aerial.

a. The volume of water is necessary to prep the insect for transition rather than the volume of the air.

b. The abdomen of the insect is designed like a star in the water as well as the air.

c. The stage of preparation in between molting is acted out in the water, while the last stage is in the air.

d. These insects breathe first in the water through gills yet continue to use the same organs to breathe in the air.

41. Which of the statements reflect information that one could reasonably infer based on the author's tone?

a. The author's tone is persuasive and attempts to call the audience to action.

b. The author's tone is passionate due to excitement over the subject and personal narrative.

c. The author's tone is informative and exhibits interest in the subject of the study.

d. The author's tone is somber, depicting some anger at the state of insect larvae.

42. Which statement best describes stoneflies, mayflies, and dragonflies?

a. They are creatures of the land and the air.

b. They have a way of protecting their spiracles when submerged.

c. Their larvae can breathe the air dissolved in water through gills of some kind.

d. The preparatory instars of these insects are aerial.

Passage #9

Questions 43–47 are based upon the following passage:

This excerpt is adaptation from "The 'Hatchery' of the Sun-Fish"--- *Scientific American,* #711

I have thought that an example of the intelligence (instinct?) of a class of fish which has come under my observation during my excursions into the Adirondack region of New York State might possibly be of interest to your readers, especially as I am not aware that any one except myself has noticed it, or, at least, has given it publicity.

The female sun-fish (called, I believe, in England, the roach or bream) makes a "hatchery" for her eggs in this wise. Selecting a spot near the banks of the numerous lakes in which this region abounds, and where the water is about 4 inches deep, and still, she builds, with her tail and snout, a circular embankment 3 inches in height and 2 thick. The circle, which is as perfect a one as could be formed with mathematical instruments, is usually a foot and a half in diameter; and at one side of this circular wall an opening is left by the fish of just sufficient width to admit her body.

The mother sun-fish, having now built or provided her "hatchery," deposits her spawn within the circular inclosure, and mounts guard at the entrance until the fry are hatched out and are sufficiently large to take charge of themselves. As the embankment, moreover, is built up to the surface of the water, no enemy can very easily obtain an entrance within the inclosure from the top; while there being only one entrance, the fish is able, with comparative ease, to keep out all intruders.

I have, as I say, noticed this beautiful instinct of the sun-fish for the perpetuity of her species more particularly in the lakes of this region; but doubtless the same habit is common to these fish in other waters.

43. What is the purpose of this passage?
   a. To show the effects of fish hatcheries on the Adirondack region
   b. To persuade the audience to study Ichthyology (fish science)
   c. To depict the sequence of mating among sun-fish
   d. To enlighten the audience on the habits of sun-fish and their hatcheries

44. What does the word *wise* in this passage most closely mean?
   a. Knowledge
   b. Manner
   c. Shrewd
   d. Ignorance

45. What is the definition of the word *fry* as it appears in the following passage?

   The mother sun-fish, having now built or provided her "hatchery," deposits her spawn within the circular inclosure, and mounts guard at the entrance until the fry are hatched out and are sufficiently large to take charge of themselves.

   a. Fish at the stage of development where they are capable of feeding themselves.
   b. Fish eggs that have been fertilized.
   c. A place where larvae is kept out of danger from other predators.
   d. A dish where fish is placed in oil and fried until golden brown.

46. How is the circle that keeps the larvae of the sun-fish made?
   a. It is formed with mathematical instruments.
   b. The sun-fish builds it with her tail and snout.
   c. It is provided to her as a "hatchery" by Mother Nature.
   d. The sun-fish builds it with her larvae.

47. The author included the third paragraph in the following passage to achieve which of the following effects?
   a. To complicate the subject matter
   b. To express a bias
   c. To insert a counterargument
   d. To conclude a sequence and add a final detail

Passage #10

In this excerpt from a novel set in nineteenth-century France, two friends, Albert de Morcef and the Count of Monte Cristo, discuss Parisian social life. Read it and answer questions 48-52.

"Mademoiselle Eugénie is pretty—I think I remember that to be her name."

"Very pretty, or rather, very beautiful," replied Albert, "but of that style of beauty which I don't appreciate; I am an ungrateful fellow."

"Really," said Monte Cristo, lowering his voice, "you don't appear to me to be very enthusiastic on the subject of this marriage."

"Mademoiselle Danglars is too rich for me," replied Morcerf, "and that frightens me."

"Bah," exclaimed Monte Cristo, "that's a fine reason to give. Are you not rich yourself?"

"My father's income is about 50,000 francs per annum; and he will give me, perhaps, ten or twelve thousand when I marry."

"That, perhaps, might not be considered a large sum, in Paris especially," said the count; "but everything doesn't depend on wealth, and it's a fine thing to have a good name, and to occupy a high station in society. Your name is celebrated, your position magnificent; and then the Comte de Morcerf is a soldier, and it's pleasing to see the integrity of a Bayard united to the poverty of a Duguesclin; disinterestedness is the brightest ray in which a noble sword can shine. As for me, I consider the union with Mademoiselle Danglars a most suitable one; she will enrich you, and you will ennoble her."

Albert shook his head and looked thoughtful. "There is still something else," said he.

"I confess," observed Monte Cristo, "that I have some difficulty in comprehending your objection to a young lady who is both rich and beautiful."

"Oh," said Morcerf, "this repugnance, if repugnance it may be called, isn't all on my side."

"Whence can it arise, then? for you told me your father desired the marriage."

"It's my mother who dissents; she has a clear and penetrating judgment and doesn't smile on the proposed union. I cannot account for it, but she seems to entertain some prejudice against the Danglars."

"Ah," said the count, in a somewhat forced tone, "that may be easily explained; the Comtesse de Morcerf, who is aristocracy and refinement itself, doesn't relish the idea of being allied by your marriage with one of ignoble birth; that is natural enough."

48. What can be inferred about Albert's family?
    a. Their finances are uncertain.
    b. Albert is the only son in his family.
    c. Their name is more respected than the Danglars'.
    d. Albert's mother and father both agree on their decisions.

49. What is Albert's attitude towards his impending marriage?
   a. Pragmatic
   b. Romantic
   c. Indifferent
   d. Apprehensive

50. What is the best description of the Count's relationship with Albert?
   a. He's like a strict parent, criticizing Albert's choices.
   b. He's like a wise uncle, giving practical advice to Albert.
   c. He's like a close friend, supporting all of Albert's opinions.
   d. He's like a suspicious investigator, asking many probing questions.

51. Which sentence is true of Albert's mother?
   a. She belongs to a noble family.
   b. She often makes poor choices.
   c. She is primarily occupied with money.
   d. She is unconcerned about her son's future.

52. Based on this passage, what is probably NOT true about French society in the 1800s?
   a. Children often received money from their parents.
   b. Marriages were sometimes arranged between families.
   c. The richest people in society were also the most respected.
   d. People were often expected to marry within their same social class.

Answer Explanations

1. C: Gulliver becomes acquainted with the people and practices of his new surroundings. Choice *C* is the correct answer because it most extensively summarizes the entire passage. While Choices *A* and *B* are reasonable possibilities, they reference portions of Gulliver's experiences, not the whole. Choice *D* is incorrect because Gulliver doesn't express repentance or sorrow in this particular passage.

2. A: Principal refers to *chief* or *primary* within the context of this text. Choice *A* is the answer that most closely aligns with this answer. Choices *B* and *D* make reference to a helper or followers while Choice *C* doesn't meet the description of Gulliver from the passage.

3. C: One can reasonably infer that Gulliver is considerably larger than the children who were playing around him because multiple children could fit into his hand. Choice *B* is incorrect because there is no indication of stress in Gulliver's tone. Choices *A* and *D* aren't the best answer because though Gulliver seems fond of his new acquaintances, he didn't travel there with the intentions of meeting new people or to express a definite love for them in this particular portion of the text.

4. C: The emperor made a *definitive decision* to expose Gulliver to their native customs. In this instance, the word *mind* was not related to a vote, question, or cognitive ability.

5. A: Choice *A* is correct. This assertion does *not* support the fact that games are a commonplace event in this culture because it mentions conduct, not games. Choices *B, C,* and *D* are incorrect because these do support the fact that games were a commonplace event.

6. B: Choice *B* is the only option that mentions the correlation between physical ability and leadership positions. Choices *A* and *D* are unrelated to physical strength and leadership abilities. Choice *C* does not make a deduction that would lead to the correct answer—it only comments upon the abilities of common townspeople.

7. D: It emphasizes Mr. Utterson's anguish in failing to identify Hyde's whereabouts. Context clues indicate that Choice *D* is correct because the passage provides great detail of Mr. Utterson's feelings about locating Hyde. Choice *A* does not fit because there is no mention of Mr. Lanyon's mental state. Choice *B* is incorrect; although the text does make mention of bells, Choice *B* is not the *best* answer overall. Choice *C* is incorrect because the passage clearly states that Mr. Utterson was determined, not unsure.

8. A: In the city. The word *city* appears in the passage several times, thus establishing the location for the reader.

9. B: It scares children. The passage states that the Juggernaut causes the children to scream. Choices *A* and *D* don't apply because the text doesn't mention either of these instances specifically. Choice *C* is incorrect because there is nothing in the text that mentions space travel.

10. B: To constantly visit. The mention of *morning, noon*, and *night* make it clear that the word *haunt* refers to frequent appearances at various locations. Choice *A* doesn't work because the text makes no mention of levitating. Choices *C* and *D* are not correct because the text makes mention of Mr. Utterson's anguish and disheartenment because of his failure to find Hyde but does not make mention of Mr. Utterson's feelings negatively affecting anyone else.

11. D: This is an example of alliteration. Choice *D* is the correct answer because of the repetition of the *L*-words. Hyperbole is an exaggeration, so Choice *A* doesn't work. No comparison is being made, so no simile or metaphor is being used, thus eliminating Choices *B* and *C*.

12. D: The speaker intends to continue to look for Hyde. Choices *A* and *B* are not possible answers because the text doesn't refer to any name changes or an identity crisis, despite Mr. Utterson's extreme obsession with finding Hyde. The text also makes no mention of a mistaken identity when referring to Hyde, so Choice *C* is also incorrect.

13. A: The tone is exasperated. While contemplative is an option because of the inquisitive nature of the text, Choice *A* is correct because the speaker is annoyed by the thought of being included when he felt that the fellow members of his race were being excluded. The speaker is not nonchalant, nor accepting of the circumstances which he describes.

14. C: Choice *C, contented,* is the only word that has different meaning. Furthermore, the speaker expresses objection and disdain throughout the entire text.

15. B: To address the feelings of exclusion expressed by African Americans after the establishment of the Fourth of July holiday. While the speaker makes biblical references, it is not the main focus of the passage, thus eliminating Choice *A* as an answer. The passage also makes no mention of wealthy landowners and doesn't speak of any positive response to the historical events, so Choices *C* and *D* are not correct.

16. D: Choice *D* is the correct answer because it clearly makes reference to justice being denied.

17. D: Hyperbole. Choices *A* and *B* are unrelated. Assonance is the repetition of sounds and commonly occurs in poetry. Parallelism refers to two statements that correlate in some manner. Choice *C* is incorrect because amplification normally refers to clarification of meaning by broadening the sentence structure, while hyperbole refers to a phrase or statement that is being exaggerated.

18. C: Display the equivocation of the speaker and those that he represents. Choice *C* is correct because the speaker is clear about his intention and stance throughout the text. Choice *A* could be true, but the words "common text" is arguable. Choice *B* is also partially true, as another group of people affected by slavery are being referenced. However, the speaker is not trying to convince the audience that injustices have been committed, as it is already understood there have been injustices committed. Choice *D* is also close to the correct answer, but it is not the *best* answer choice possible.

19. B: A period of time. It is apparent that Lincoln is referring to a period of time within the context of the passage because of how the sentence is structured with the word *ago*.

20. C: Lincoln's reference to *the brave men, living and dead, who struggled here,* proves that he is referring to a battlefield. Choices *A* and *B* are incorrect, as a *civil war* is mentioned and not a war with France or a war in the Sahara Desert. Choice *D* is incorrect because it does not make sense to consecrate a President's ground instead of a battlefield ground for soldiers who died during the American Civil War.

21. D: Abraham Lincoln is the former president of the United States, and he references a "civil war" during his address.

22. A: The audience should consider the death of the people that fought in the war as an example and perpetuate the ideals of freedom that the soldiers died fighting for. Lincoln doesn't address any of the topics outlined in Choices *B, C,* or *D*. Therefore, Choice *A* is the correct answer.

23. D: Choice *D* is the correct answer because of the repetition of the word *people* at the end of the passage. Choice *A*, *antimetabole*, is the repetition of words in a succession. Choice *B*, *antiphrasis*, is a form of denial of an assertion in a text. Choice *C*, *anaphora*, is the repetition that occurs at the beginning of sentences.

24. A: Choice *A* is correct because Lincoln's intention was to memorialize the soldiers who had fallen as a result of war as well as celebrate those who had put their lives in danger for the sake of their country. Choices *B* and *D* are incorrect because Lincoln's speech was supposed to foster a sense of pride among the members of the audience while connecting them to the soldiers' experiences.

25. A: The word *patronage* most nearly means *auspices*, which means *protection* or *support*. Choice *B*, *aberration*, means *deformity* and does not make sense within the context of the sentence. Choice *C*, *acerbic,* means *bitter* and also does not make sense in the sentence. Choice *D*, *adulation*, is a positive word meaning *praise*, and thus does not fit with the word *condescending* in the sentence.

26. D: *Working man* is most closely aligned with Choice *D*, *bourgeois.* In the context of the speech, the word *bourgeois* means *working* or *middle class*. Choice *A*, *plebian*, does suggest *common people*; however, this is a term that is specific to ancient Rome. Choice *B***,** *viscount*, is a European title used to describe a specific degree of nobility. Choice *C*, *entrepreneur*, is a person who operates their own business.

27. C: In the context of the speech, the term *working man* most closely correlates with Choice *C*, *working man is someone who works for wages among the middle class.* Choice *A* is not mentioned in the passage and is off-topic. Choice *B* may be true in some cases, but it does not reflect the sentiment described for the term *working man* in the passage. Choice *D* may also be arguably true. However, it is not given as a definition but as *acts* of the working man, and the topics of *field, factory,* and *screen* are not mentioned in the passage.

28. D: *Enterprise* most closely means *cause*. Choices *A, B,* and *C* are all related to the term *enterprise*. However, Dickens speaks of a *cause* here, not a company, courage, or a game. *He will stand by such an enterprise* is a call to stand by a cause to enable the working man to have a certain autonomy over his own economic standing. The very first paragraph ends with the statement that the working man *shall . . . have a share in the management of an institution which is designed for his benefit.*

29. B: The speaker's salutation is one from an entertainer to his audience and uses the friendly language to connect to his audience before a serious speech. Recall in the first paragraph that the speaker is there to "accompany [the audience] . . . through one of my little Christmas books," making him an author there to entertain the crowd with his own writing. The speech preceding the reading is the passage itself, and, as the tone indicates, a serious speech addressing the "working man." Although the passage speaks of employers and employees, the speaker himself is not an employer of the audience, so Choice *A* is incorrect. Choice *C* is also incorrect, as the salutation is not used ironically, but sincerely, as the speech addresses the wellbeing of the crowd. Choice *D* is incorrect because the speech is not given by a politician, but by a writer.

30. B: For the working man to have a say in his institution which is designed for his benefit. Choice *A* is incorrect because that is the speaker's *first* desire, not his second. Choices *C* and *D* are tricky because the language of both of these is mentioned after the word *second*. However, the speaker doesn't get to the second wish until the next sentence. Choices *C* and *D* are merely prepositions preparing for the statement of the main clause, Choice *B*.

31. D: The use of "I" could have all of the effects for the reader; it could serve to have a "hedging" effect, allow the reader to connect with the author in a more personal way, and cause the reader to empathize more with the egrets. However, it doesn't distance the reader from the text, thus eliminating Choice *D*.

32. C: The quote provides an example of a warden protecting one of the colonies. Choice *A* is incorrect because the speaker of the quote is a warden, not a hunter. Choice *B* is incorrect because the quote does not lighten the mood but shows the danger of the situation between the wardens and the hunters. Choice *D* is incorrect because there is no humor found in the quote.

33. D: A *rookery* is a colony of breeding birds. Although *rookery* could mean Choice *A*, houses in a slum area, it does not make sense in this context. Choices *B* and *C* are both incorrect, as this is not a place for hunters to trade tools or for wardens to trade stories.

34. B: An important bird colony. The previous sentence is describing "twenty colonies" of birds, so what follows should be a bird colony. Choice *A* may be true, but we have no evidence of this in the text. Choice *C* does touch on the tension between the hunters and wardens, but there is no official "Bird Island Battle" mentioned in the text. Choice *D* does not exist in the text.

35. D: To demonstrate the success of the protective work of the Audubon Association. The text mentions several different times how and why the association has been successful and gives examples to back this fact. Choice *A* is incorrect because although the article, in some instances, calls certain people to act, it is not the purpose of the entire passage. There is no way to tell if Choices *B* and *C* are correct, as they are not mentioned in the text.

36. C: To have a better opportunity to hunt the birds. Choice *A* might be true in a general sense, but it is not relevant to the context of the text. Choice *B* is incorrect because the hunters are not studying lines of flight to help wardens, but to hunt birds. Choice *D* is incorrect because nothing in the text mentions that hunters are trying to build homes underneath lines of flight of birds for good luck.

37. A: It introduces certain insects that transition from water to air. Choice *B* is incorrect because although the passage talks about gills, it is not the central idea of the passage. Choices *C* and *D* are incorrect because the passage does not "define" or "invite," but only serves as an introduction to stoneflies, dragonflies, and mayflies and their transition from water to air.

38. C: The act of shedding part or all of the outer shell. Choices *A*, *B*, and *D* are incorrect.

39. B: The first paragraph serves as a contrast to the second. Notice how the first paragraph goes into detail describing how insects are able to breathe air. The second paragraph acts as a contrast to the first by stating "[i]t is of great interest to find that, nevertheless, a number of insects spend much of their time under water." Watch for transition words such as "nevertheless" to help find what type of passage you're dealing with.

40: C: The stage of preparation in between molting is acted out in the water, while the last stage is in the air. Choices *A, B,* and *D* are all incorrect. *Instars* is the phase between two periods of molting, and the text explains when these transitions occur.

41. C: The author's tone is informative and exhibits interest in the subject of the study. Overall, the author presents us with information on the subject. One moment where personal interest is depicted is when the author states, "It is of great interest to find that, nevertheless, a number of insects spend much of their time under water."

42. C: Their larva can breathe the air dissolved in water through gills of some kind. This is stated in the last paragraph. Choice *A* is incorrect because the text mentions this in a general way at the beginning of the passage concerning "insects as a whole." Choice *B* is incorrect because this is stated of beetles and water-bugs, and not the insects in question. Choice *D* is incorrect because this is the opposite of what the text says of instars.

43. D: To enlighten the audience on the habits of sun-fish and their hatcheries. Choice *A* is incorrect because although the Adirondack region is mentioned in the text, there is no cause or effect relationships between the region and fish hatcheries depicted here. Choice *B* is incorrect because the text does not have an agenda, but rather is meant to inform the audience. Finally, Choice *C* is incorrect because the text says nothing of how sun-fish mate.

44. B: The word *wise* in this passage most closely means *manner*. Choices *A* and *C* are synonyms of *wise*; however, they are not relevant in the context of the text. Choice *D*, *ignorance*, is opposite of the word *wise*, and is therefore incorrect.

45. A: Fish at the stage of development where they are capable of feeding themselves. Even if the word *fry* isn't immediately known to the reader, the context gives a hint when it says "until the fry are hatched out and are sufficiently large to take charge of themselves."

46. B: The sun-fish builds it with her tail and snout. The text explains this in the second paragraph: "she builds, with her tail and snout, a circular embankment 3 inches in height and 2 thick." Choice *A* is used in the text as a simile.

47. D: To conclude a sequence and add a final detail. The concluding sequence is expressed in the phrase "[t]he mother sun-fish, having now built or provided her 'hatchery.'" The final detail is the way in which the sun-fish guards the "inclosure." Choices *A, B,* and *C* are incorrect.

48. C: Their name is more respected than the Danglars'. This inference question can be answered by eliminating incorrect answers. Choice *A* is tempting, considering that Albert mentions money as a concern in his marriage. However, although he may not be as rich as his fiancée, his father still has a stable income of 50,000 francs a year. Choice *B* isn't mentioned at all in the passage, so it's impossible to make an inference. Finally, Choice *D* is clearly false because Albert's father arranged his marriage but his mother doesn't approve of it. Evidence for Choice *C* can be found in the Count's comparison of Albert and Eugénie: "she will enrich you, and you will ennoble her." In other words, the Danglars are wealthier but the Morcef family has a more noble background.

49. D: Apprehensive. As in question 7, there are many clues in the passage that indicate Albert's attitude towards his marriage—far from enthusiastic, he has many reservations. This question requires test takers to understand the vocabulary in the answer choices. "Pragmatic" is closest in meaning to "realistic," and "indifferent" means "uninterested." The only word related to feeling worried, uncertain, or unfavorable about the future is "apprehensive."

50. B: He is like a wise uncle, giving practical advice to Albert. Choice *A* is incorrect because the Count's tone is friendly and conversational. Choice *C* is also incorrect because the Count questions why Albert doesn't want to marry a young, beautiful, and rich girl. While the Count asks many questions, he isn't particularly "probing" or "suspicious"—instead, he's asking to find out more about Albert's situation and then give him advice about marriage.

51. A: She belongs to a noble family. Though Albert's mother doesn't appear in the scene, there's more than enough information to answer this question. More than once is his family's noble background mentioned (not to mention that Albert's mother is the Comtess de Morcef, a noble title). The other answer choices can be eliminated—she is obviously deeply concerned about her son's future; money isn't her highest priority because otherwise she would favor a marriage with the wealthy Danglars; and Albert describes her "clear and penetrating judgment," meaning she makes good decisions.

52. C: The richest people in society were also the most respected. The Danglars family is wealthier but the Morcef family has a more aristocratic name, which gives them a higher social standing. Evidence for the other answer choices can be found throughout the passage: Albert mentioned receiving money from his father's fortune after his marriage; Albert's father has arranged this marriage for him; and the Count speculates that Albert's mother disapproves of this marriage because Eugénie isn't from a noble background like the Morcef family, implying that she would prefer a match with a girl from aristocratic society.

Writing and Language

The Writing and Language section of the SAT presents passages with deliberate errors; the section is designed to assess the test taker's command of standard conventions of English Language and his or her ability to edit errors appropriately. While questions will ask test takers to select more effective alternatives to given sentences and revise and edit errors, they will not require test takers to identify specific grammatical rules.

The section includes four passages, each of approximately 400-450 words in length. There is one passage dedicated to each of the following four categories: careers, science, humanities, and social studies. Careers passages present trends or debates in various industries like technology, communications, or healthcare. Science passages are drawn from topics in earth science, chemistry, biology, or physics. Humanities passages may focus on any number of topics such as arts, literature, dance, or music. Social studies passages may pull topics from a variety of areas including history, sociology, psychology, anthropology, and political science. All of the information needed to answer the questions is provided within the passages and test takers do not need to have prior knowledge of the passages' content to obtain the correct answers.

Test takers are given 35 minutes to read the four passages and then answer a total of 44 multiple-choice questions—eleven per passage. In addition to surveying the test taker's ability to comprehend and revise passages about various topics, the section tests one's skill in understanding various writing styles. The test taker will encounter at least one passage written in one of three different writing styles: narrative, argumentative, and explanatory or informative. In addition, test takers can expect to interpret graphs, tables, charts, or other graphics that, in some way, support factual content or an opinion presented in the graphic's passage. After reading the passage and reviewing the graphic, test takers may be asked to correct an error in the passage that contradicts information presented in the graphic. Alternatively, they may need to use information gleaned from the graphic to select a more specific description for part or all of the passage in place of the vague description originally provided. Essentially, the passage may misinterpret the graphic or the graphic may otherwise illuminate important data or facts that can strengthen the argument or explanation in the passage; test takers will be required to identify these findings.

Passages and the questions pertaining to them usually appear side by side on the test, with the passage on the left side of the page and the questions on the right. Some or all passages may span multiple pages, so test takers should ensure they have read the entire passage before answering questions that pertain to the passage in its entirety. In contrast, some test takers find it useful to answer questions addressing specific points or details as that information is encountered in the passage; question numbers embedded within the passage should be used to guide the test taker to the section of the passage for which a question pertains. Test takers should then carefully read the underlined text in the passage following the number and determine if errors are present. The related question will then ask test takers to consider the underlined sentence or section and the provided answer choices. Test takers must select the answer choice that offers that best revision or most effective replacement for the underlined section. If the original sentence seems correct as is, test takers should select Choice *A*—NO CHANGE—which represents that the initial sentence was free from errors and should remain unchanged.

Underlined text will not necessarily follow all of the embedded boxed numbers in the passage. In these situations, test takers should still use the boxed number to guide their attention to the pertinent question, and then the appropriate question will inform them on what to do. Some sentences or paragraphs may be numbered, and test takers will have to decide how that text should be ordered or where a particular sentence or paragraph should be inserted.

There are two principle question types on the Writing and Language Section. For the Expression of Ideas questions, test takers will select answers that improve the text's organization, topic development, and the effectiveness of the language used. The scope of these questions assesses one's understanding of text structure and organization, ability to analyze evidence and arguments and strengthen them with designated improvements, and his or her specific skills in comprehending passages addressing topics in science, history, and the humanities. Standard English Convention questions address one's skill in identifying and correcting errors in sentence structure, word usage, grammar, and punctuation. These questions evaluate the test taker's skill in determining the correct meaning of words in context, selecting precise words, and revising text to be more concise, coherent, and consistent in tone and style.

While the vast majority of questions in the Writing and Language section are comprised of these two question types in roughly equal proportions, as mentioned, a small number of questions will also assess the test taker's ability to interpret graph, tables, and charts. For this reason, in addition to studying grammatical rules, vocabulary, and word usage and developing writing skills and an eye and ear for issues with organization and flow, test takers should practice reading and interpreting tables, graphs, and charts. As such. the sections that follow provide a review of material pertinent to success in this section, covering topics on English language conventions, text structure and readability, syntax and grammar, analyzing opinions and facts, and interpreting graphics.

Expression of Ideas

This Writing and Language section is about *how* the information is communicated rather than the subject matter itself. The good news is there isn't any writing! Instead, it's like being an editor helping the writer find the best ways to express their ideas. Things to consider include: how well a topic is developed, how accurately facts are presented, whether the writing flows logically and cohesively, and how effectively the writer uses language. This can seem like a lot to remember, but these concepts are the same ones taught way back in elementary school.

One last thing to remember while going through this guide is not to be intimidated by the terminology. Phrases like "pronoun-antecedent agreement" and "possessive determiners" can sound confusing and complicated, but the ideas are often quite simple and easy to understand. Though proper terminology is used to explain the rules and guidelines, the SAT Writing and Language Test is not a technical grammar test.

Organization

Good writing is not merely a random collection of sentences. No matter how well written, sentences must relate and coordinate appropriately to one another. If not, the writing seems random, haphazard, and disorganized. Therefore, good writing must be *organized* (where each sentence fits a larger context and relates to the sentences around it).

<u>Transition Words</u>
The writer should act as a guide, showing the reader how all the sentences fit together. Consider this example:

> Seat belts save more lives than any other automobile safety feature. Many studies show that airbags save lives as well. Not all cars have airbags. Many older cars don't. Air bags aren't

entirely reliable. Studies show that in 15% of accidents, airbags don't deploy as designed. Seat belt malfunctions are extremely rare.

There's nothing wrong with any of these sentences individually, but together they're disjointed and difficult to follow. The best way for the writer to communicate information is through the use of *transition words*. Here are examples of transition words and phrases that tie sentences together, enabling a more natural flow:

- To show causality: as a result, therefore, and consequently
- To compare and contrast: *however, but*, and *on the other hand*
- To introduce examples: *for instance, namely*, and *including*
- To show order of importance: *foremost, primarily, secondly*, and *lastly*

The above is not a complete list of transitions. There are many more that can be used; however, most fit into these or similar categories. The important point is that the words should clearly show the relationship between sentences, supporting information, and the main idea.

Here is an update to the previous example using transition words. These changes make it easier to read and bring clarity to the writer's points:

> Seat belts save more lives than any other automobile safety feature. Many studies show that airbags save lives as well. However, not all cars have airbags. For instance, some older cars don't. Furthermore, air bags aren't entirely reliable. For example, studies show that in 15% of accidents, airbags don't deploy as designed. But, on the other hand, seat belt malfunctions are extremely rare.

Also, be prepared to analyze whether the writer is using the best transition word or phrase for the situation. Take this sentence for example: "As a result, seat belt malfunctions are extremely rare." This sentence doesn't make sense in the context above because the writer is trying to show the *contrast* between seat belts and airbags, not the causality.

<u>Logical Sequence</u>

Even if the writer includes plenty of information to support their point, the writing is only effective when the information is in a logical order. *Logical sequencing* is really just common sense, but it's an important writing technique. First, the writer should introduce the main idea, whether for a paragraph, a section, or the entire piece. Then they should present evidence to support the main idea by using transitional language. This shows the reader how the information relates to the main idea and to the sentences around it. The writer should then take time to interpret the information, making sure necessary connections are obvious to the reader. Finally, the writer can summarize the information in a closing section.

Although most writing follows this pattern, it isn't a set rule. Sometimes writers change the order for effect. For example, the writer can begin with a surprising piece of supporting information to grab the reader's attention, and then transition to the main idea. Thus, if a passage doesn't follow the logical order, don't immediately assume it's wrong. However, most writing usually settles into a logical sequence after a nontraditional beginning.

Focus

Good writing stays *focused* and on topic. During the test, determine the main idea for each passage and then look for times when the writer strays from the point they're trying to make. Let's go back to the seat belt example. If the writer suddenly begins talking about how well airbags, crumple zones, or other safety features work to save lives, they might be losing focus from the topic of "safety belts."

Focus can also refer to individual sentences. Sometimes the writer does address the main topic, but in a confusing way. For example:

> Thanks to seat belt usage, survival in serious car accidents has shown a consistently steady increase since the development of the retractable seat belt in the 1950s.

This statement is definitely on topic, but it's not easy to follow. A simpler, more focused version of this sentence might look like this:

> Seat belts have consistently prevented car fatalities since the 1950s.

Providing *adequate information* is another aspect of focused writing. Statements like "seat belts are important" and "many people drive cars" are true, but they're so general that they don't contribute much to the writer's case. When reading a passage, watch for these kinds of unfocused statements.

Introductions and Conclusions

Examining the writer's strategies for introductions and conclusions puts the reader in the right mindset to interpret the rest of the passage. Look for methods the writer might use for introductions such as:

- Stating the main point immediately, followed by outlining how the rest of the piece supports this claim.
- Establishing important, smaller pieces of the main idea first, and then grouping these points into a case for the main idea.
- Opening with a quotation, anecdote, question, seeming paradox, or other piece of interesting information, and then using it to lead to the main point.

Whatever method the writer chooses, the introduction should make their intention clear, establish their voice as a credible one, and encourage a person to continue reading.

Conclusions tend to follow a similar pattern. In them, the writer restates their main idea a final time, often after summarizing the smaller pieces of that idea. If the introduction uses a quote or anecdote to grab the reader's attention, the conclusion often makes reference to it again. Whatever way the writer chooses to arrange the conclusion, the final restatement of the main idea should be clear and simple for the reader to interpret.

Finally, conclusions shouldn't introduce any new information.

Precision

People often think of *precision* in terms of math, but precise word choice is another key to successful writing. Since language itself is imprecise, it's important for the writer to find the exact word or words to convey the full, intended meaning of a given situation. For example:

> The number of deaths has gone down since seat belt laws started.

There are several problems with this sentence. First, the word *deaths* is too general. From the context, it's assumed that the writer is referring only to *deaths* caused by car accidents. However, without clarification, the sentence lacks impact and is probably untrue. The phrase "gone down" might be accurate, but a more precise word could provide more information and greater accuracy. Did the numbers show a slow and steady decrease of highway fatalities or a sudden drop? If the latter is true, the writer is missing a chance to make their point more dramatically. Instead of "gone down" they could substitute *plummeted, fallen drastically*, or *rapidly diminished* to bring the information to life. Also, the phrase "seat belt laws" is unclear. Does it refer to laws requiring cars to include seat belts or to laws requiring drivers and passengers to use them? Finally, *started* is not a strong verb. Words like *enacted* or *adopted* are more direct and make the content more real. When put together, these changes create a far more powerful sentence:

> The number of highway fatalities has plummeted since laws requiring seat belt usage were enacted.

However, it's important to note that precise word choice can sometimes be taken too far. If the writer of the sentence above takes precision to an extreme, it might result in the following:

> The incidence of high-speed, automobile accident related fatalities has decreased 75% and continued to remain at historical lows since the initial set of federal legislations requiring seat belt use were enacted in 1992.

This sentence is extremely precise, but it takes so long to achieve that precision that it suffers from a lack of clarity. Precise writing is about finding the right balance between information and flow. This is also an issue of *conciseness* (discussed in the next section).

The last thing to consider with precision is a word choice that's not only unclear or uninteresting, but also confusing or misleading. For example:

> The number of highway fatalities has become hugely lower since laws requiring seat belt use were enacted.

In this case, the reader might be confused by the word *hugely*. Huge means large, but here the writer uses *hugely* to describe something small. Though most readers can decipher this, doing so disconnects them from the flow of the writing and makes the writer's point less effective.

On the test, there can be questions asking for alternatives to the writer's word choice. In answering these questions, always consider the context and look for a balance between precision and flow.

Conciseness

"Less is more" is a good rule to follow when writing a sentence. Unfortunately, writers often include extra words and phrases that seem necessary at the time but add nothing to the main idea. This confuses the reader and creates unnecessary repetition. Writing that lacks *conciseness* is usually guilty of excessive wordiness and redundant phrases. Here's an example containing both of these issues:

> When legislators decided to begin creating legislation making it mandatory for automobile drivers and passengers to make use of seat belts while in cars, a large number of them made those laws for reasons that were political reasons.

There are several empty or "fluff" words here that take up too much space. These can be eliminated while still maintaining the writer's meaning. For example:

- "decided to begin" could be shortened to "began"
- "making it mandatory for" could be shortened to "requiring"
- "make use of" could be shortened to "use"
- "a large number" could be shortened to "many"

In addition, there are several examples of redundancy that can be eliminated:

- "legislators decided to begin creating legislation" and "made those laws"
- "automobile drivers and passengers" and "while in cars"
- "reasons that were political reasons"

These changes are incorporated as follows:

> When legislators began requiring drivers and passengers to use seat belts, many of them did so for political reasons.

There are many examples of redundant phrases, such as "add an additional," "complete and total," "time schedule," and "transportation vehicle." If asked to identify a redundant phrase on the test, look for words that are close together with the same (or similar) meanings.

Proposition

The *proposition* (also called the *claim* since it can be true or false) is a clear statement of the point or idea the writer is trying to make. The length or format of a proposition can vary, but it often takes the form of a *topic sentence*. A good topic sentence is:

- Clear: does not weave a complicated web of words for the reader to decode or unwrap

- Concise: presents only the information needed to make the claim and doesn't clutter up the statement with unnecessary details

- Precise: clarifies the exact point the writer wants to make and doesn't use broad, overreaching statements

Look at the following example:

> The civil rights movement, from its genesis in the Emancipation Proclamation to its current struggles with de facto discrimination, has changed the face of the United States more than any other factor in its history.

Is the statement clear? Yes, the statement is fairly clear, although other words can be substituted for "genesis" and "de facto" to make it easier to understand.

Is the statement concise? No, the statement is not concise. Details about the Emancipation Proclamation and the current state of the movement are unnecessary for a topic sentence. Those details should be saved for the body of the text.

Is the statement precise? No, the statement is not precise. What exactly does the writer mean by "changed the face of the United States"? The writer should be more specific about the effects of the movement. Also, suggesting that something has a greater impact than anything else in U.S. history is far too ambitious a statement to make.

A better version might look like this:

> The civil rights movement has greatly increased the career opportunities available for African-Americans.

The unnecessary language and details are removed, and the claim can now be measured and supported.

Support

Once the main idea or proposition is stated, the writer attempts to prove or *support* the claim with text evidence and supporting details.

Take for example the sentence, "Seat belts save lives." Though most people can't argue with this statement, its impact on the reader is much greater when supported by additional content. The writer can support this idea by:

- Providing statistics on the rate of highway fatalities alongside statistics for estimated seat belt usage.
- Explaining the science behind a car accident and what happens to a passenger who doesn't use a seat belt.
- Offering anecdotal evidence or true stories from reliable sources on how seat belts prevent fatal injuries in car crashes.

However, using only one form of supporting evidence is not nearly as effective as using a variety to support a claim. Presenting only a list of statistics can be boring to the reader but providing a true story that's both interesting and humanizing helps. In addition, one example isn't always enough to prove the writer's larger point, so combining it with other examples is extremely effective for the writing. Thus, when reading a passage, don't just look for a single form of supporting evidence.

Another key aspect of supporting evidence is a *reliable source*. Does the writer include the source of the information? If so, is the source well known and trustworthy? Is there a potential for bias? For example, a seat belt study done by a seat belt manufacturer may have its own agenda to promote.

Effective Language Use

Language can be analyzed in a variety of ways. But one of the primary ways is its effectiveness in communicating and especially convincing others.

Rhetoric is a literary technique used to make the writing (or speaking) more effective or persuasive. Rhetoric makes us of other effective language devices such as irony, metaphors, allusion, and repetition. An example of the rhetorical use of repetition would be: "Let go, I say, let go!!!".

Figures of Speech

A *figure of speech* (sometimes called an *idiom*) is a rhetorical device. It's a phrase that's not intended to be taken literally.

When the writer uses a figure of speech, their intention must be clear if it's to be used effectively. Some phrases can be interpreted in a number of ways, causing confusion for the reader. In the SAT Writing and Language Test, questions may ask for an alternative to a problematic word or phrase. Look for clues to the writer's true intention to determine the best replacement. Likewise, some figures of speech may seem out of place in a more formal piece of writing. To show this, here is the previous seat belt example but with one slight change:

> Seat belts save more lives than any other automobile safety feature. Many studies show that airbags save lives as well. However, not all cars have airbags. For instance, some older cars don't. In addition, air bags aren't entirely reliable. For example, studies show that in 15% of accidents, airbags don't deploy as designed. But, on the other hand, seat belt malfunctions happen once in a blue moon.

Most people know that "once in a blue moon" refers to something that rarely happens. However, because the rest of the paragraph is straightforward and direct, using this figurative phrase distracts the reader. In this example, the earlier version is much more effective.

Now it's important to take a moment and review the meaning of the word *literally*. This is because it's one of the most misunderstood and misused words in the English language. *Literally* means that something is exactly what it says it is, and there can be no interpretation or exaggeration. Unfortunately, *literally* is often used for emphasis as in the following example:

> This morning, I literally couldn't get out of bed.

This sentence meant to say that the person was extremely tired and wasn't able to get up. However, the sentence can't *literally* be true unless that person was tied down to the bed, paralyzed, or affected by a strange situation that the writer (most likely) didn't intend. Here's another example:

> I literally died laughing.

The writer tried to say that something was very funny. However, unless they're writing this from beyond the grave, it can't *literally* be true.

Rhetorical Fallacies

A *rhetorical fallacy* is an argument that doesn't make sense. It usually involves distracting the reader from the issue at hand in some way. There are many kinds of rhetorical fallacies. Here are just a few, along with examples of each:

- *Ad Hominem*: Makes an irrelevant attack against the person making the claim, rather than addressing the claim itself.
- Senator Wilson opposed the new seat belt legislation, but should we really listen to someone who's been divorced four times?

- *Exaggeration*: Represents an idea or person in an obviously excessive manner.
- Senator Wilson opposed the new seat belt legislation. Maybe she thinks if more people die in car accidents, it will help with overpopulation.
- *Stereotyping (or Categorical Claim)*: Claims that all people of a certain group are the same in some way.
- Senator Wilson still opposes the new seat belt legislation. You know women can never admit when they're wrong.

When examining a possible rhetorical fallacy, carefully consider the point the writer is trying to make and if the argument directly relates to that point. If something feels wrong, there's a good chance that a fallacy is at play. The SAT Writing and Language section doesn't expect the fallacy to be named using specific terms like those above. However, questions can include identifying why something is a fallacy or suggesting a sounder argument.

Style, Tone, and Mood

Style, *tone*, and *mood* are often thought to be the same thing. Though they're closely related, there are important differences to keep in mind. The easiest way to do this is to remember that style "creates and affects" tone and mood. More specifically, style is *how the writer uses words* to create the desired tone and mood for their writing.

<u>Style</u>
Style can include any number of technical writing choices, and some may have to be analyzed on the test. A few examples of style choices include:

- Sentence Construction: When presenting facts, does the writer use shorter sentences to create a quicker sense of the supporting evidence, or do they use longer sentences to elaborate and explain the information?
- Technical Language: Does the writer use jargon to demonstrate their expertise in the subject, or do they use ordinary language to help the reader understand things in simple terms?
- Formal Language: Does the writer refrain from using contractions such as won't or can't to create a more formal tone, or do they use a colloquial, conversational style to connect to the reader?
- Formatting: Does the writer use a series of shorter paragraphs to help the reader follow a line of argument, or do they use longer paragraphs to examine an issue in great detail and demonstrate their knowledge of the topic?

On the test, examine the writer's style and how their writing choices affect the way the passage comes across.

<u>Tone</u>
Tone refers to the writer's attitude toward the subject matter. Tone is usually explained in terms of a work of fiction. For example, the tone conveys how the writer feels about their characters and the situations in which they're involved. Nonfiction writing is sometimes thought to have no tone at all, but this is incorrect.

A lot of nonfiction writing has a neutral tone, which is an extremely important tone for the writer to take. A neutral tone demonstrates that the writer is presenting a topic impartially and letting the information speak for itself. On the other hand, nonfiction writing can be just as effective and appropriate if the tone isn't neutral. For instance, take the previous examples involving seat belt use. In them, the writer mostly chooses to retain a neutral tone when presenting information. If the writer would instead include their own personal experience of losing a friend or family member in a car accident, the tone would change dramatically. The tone would no longer be neutral. Now it would show that the writer has a personal stake in the content, allowing them to interpret the information in a different way. When analyzing tone, consider what the writer is trying to achieve in the passage, and how they *create* the tone using style.

Mood

Mood refers to the feelings and atmosphere that the writer's words create for the reader. Like tone, many nonfiction pieces can have a neutral mood. To return to the previous example, if the writer would choose to include information about a person they know being killed in a car accident, the passage would suddenly carry an emotional component that is absent in the previous examples. Depending on how they present the information, the writer can create a sad, angry, or even hopeful mood. When analyzing the mood, consider what the writer wants to accomplish and whether the best choice was made to achieve that end.

Consistency

Whatever style, tone, and mood the writer uses, good writing should remain *consistent* throughout. If the writer chooses to include the tragic, personal experience above, it would affect the style, tone, and mood of the entire piece. It would seem out of place for such an example to be used in the middle of a neutral, measured, and analytical piece. To adjust the rest of the piece, the writer needs to make additional choices to remain consistent. For example, the writer might decide to use the word *tragedy* in place of the more neutral *fatality*, or they could describe a series of car-related deaths as an *epidemic*. Adverbs and adjectives such as *devastating* or *horribly* could be included to maintain this consistent attitude toward the content. When analyzing writing, look for sudden shifts in style, tone, and mood, and consider whether the writer would be wiser to maintain the prevailing strategy.

Syntax

Syntax is the order of words in a sentence. While most of the writing on the test has proper syntax, there may be questions on ways to vary the syntax for effectiveness. One of the easiest writing mistakes to spot is *repetitive sentence structure*. For example:

> Seat belts are important. They save lives. People don't like to use them. We have to pass seat belt laws. Then more people will wear seat belts. More lives will be saved.

What's the first thing that comes to mind when reading this example? The short, choppy, and repetitive sentences! In fact, most people notice this syntax issue more than the content itself. By combining some sentences and changing the syntax of others, the writer can create a more effective writing passage:

> Seat belts are important because they save lives. Since people don't like to use seat belts, though, more laws requiring their usage need to be passed. Only then will more people wear them and only then will more lives be saved.

Many rhetorical devices can be used to vary syntax (more than can possibly be named here). These often have intimidating names like *anadiplosis*, *metastasis*, and *paremptosis*. The test questions don't ask for definitions of these tricky techniques, but they can ask how the writer plays with the words and what effect that has on the writing. For example, *anadiplosis* is when the last word (or phrase) from a sentence is used to begin the next sentence:

Cars are driven by people. People cause accidents. Accidents cost taxpayers money.

The test doesn't ask for this technique by name but be prepared to recognize what the writer is doing and why they're using the technique in this situation. In this example, the writer is probably using *anadiplosis* to demonstrate causation.

Quantitative Information

As mentioned, some passages in the test contains *infographics* such as charts, tables, or graphs. In these cases, interpret the information presented and determine how well it supports the claims made in the text. For example, if the writer makes a case that seat belts save more lives than other automobile safety measures, they might want to include a graph (like the one below) showing the number of lives saved by seat belts versus those saved by air bags.

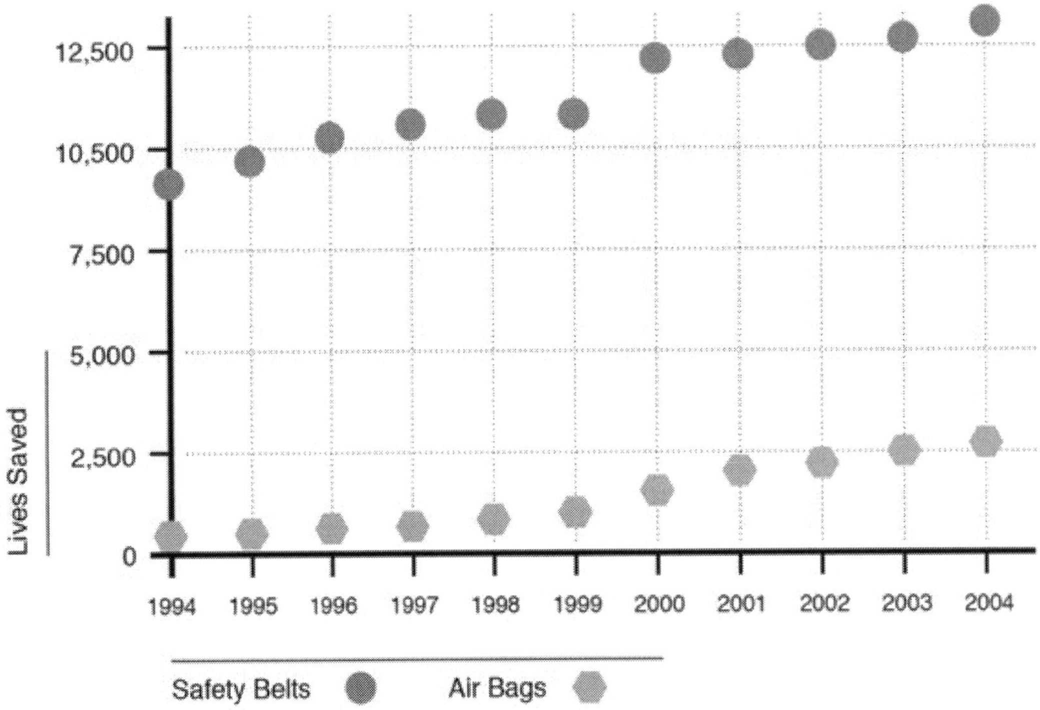

Based on data from the National Highway Traffic Safety Administration

If the graph clearly shows a higher number of lives are saved by seat belts, then it's effective. However, if the graph shows air bags save more lives than seat belts, then it doesn't support the writer's case.

Finally, graphs should be easy to understand. Their information should immediately be clear to the reader at a glance. Here are some basic things to keep in mind when interpreting infographics:

- In a *bar graph*, higher bars represent larger numbers. Lower bars represent smaller numbers.
- *Line graphs* are the same, but often show trends over time. A line that consistently ascends from left to right shows a steady increase over time. A line that consistently descends from left to right shows a steady decrease over time. If the line bounces up and down, this represents instability or inconsistency in the trend. When interpreting a line graph, determine the point the writer is trying to make, and then see if the graph supports that point.
- *Pie charts* are used to show proportions or percentages of a whole but are less effective in showing change over time.
- *Tables* present information in numerical form, not as graphics. When interpreting a table, make sure to look for patterns in the numbers.

There can also be timelines, illustrations, or maps on the test. When interpreting these, keep in mind the writer's intentions and determine whether or not the graphic supports the case.

Standard English Conventions

Types of Sentences

There isn't an overabundance of absolutes in grammar, but here is one: every sentence in the English language falls into one of four categories.

- Declarative: a simple statement that ends with a period

  The price of milk per gallon is the same as the price of gasoline.

- Imperative: a command, instruction, or request that ends with a period

  Buy milk when you stop to fill up your car with gas.

- Interrogative: a question that ends with a question mark

  Will you buy the milk?

- Exclamatory: a statement or command that expresses emotions like anger, urgency, or surprise and ends with an exclamation mark

  Buy the milk now!

Declarative sentences are the most common type, probably because they are comprised of the most general content, without any of the bells and whistles that the other three types contain. They are, simply, declarations or statements of any degree of seriousness, importance, or information.

Imperative sentences often seem to be missing a subject. The subject is there, though; it is just not visible or audible because it is *implied*. Look at the imperative example sentence.

Buy the milk when you fill up your car with gas.

You is the implied subject, the one to whom the command is issued. This is sometimes called *the understood you* because it is understood that *you* is the subject of the sentence.

Interrogative sentences—those that ask questions—are defined as such from the idea of the word *interrogation*, the action of questions being asked of suspects by investigators. Although that is serious business, interrogative sentences apply to all kinds of questions.

To exclaim is at the root of *exclamatory* sentences. These are made with strong emotions behind them. The only technical difference between a declarative or imperative sentence and an exclamatory one is the exclamation mark at the end. The example declarative and imperative sentences can both become an exclamatory one simply by putting an exclamation mark at the end of the sentences.

> The price of milk per gallon is the same as the price of gasoline!
> Buy milk when you stop to fill up your car with gas!

After all, someone might be really excited by the price of gas or milk, or they could be mad at the person that will be buying the milk! However, as stated before, exclamation marks in abundance defeat their own purpose! After a while, they begin to cause fatigue! When used only for their intended purpose, they can have their expected and desired effect.

Parts of Speech

<u>Nouns</u>
A noun is a person, place, thing, or idea. All nouns fit into one of two types, common or proper.

A *common noun* is a word that identifies any of a class of people, places, or things. Examples include numbers, objects, animals, feelings, concepts, qualities, and actions. *A, an,* or *the* usually precedes the common noun. These parts of speech are called *articles*. Here are some examples of sentences using nouns preceded by articles.

> *A* building is under construction.
> *The* girl would like to move to *the* city.

A *proper noun* (also called a *proper name*) is used for the specific name of an individual person, place, or organization. The first letter in a proper noun is capitalized. "My name is *Mary*." "I work for *Walmart*."

Nouns sometimes serve as adjectives (which themselves describe nouns), such as "hockey player" and "state government."

An abstract noun is an idea, state, or quality. It is something that can't be touched, such as happiness, courage, evil, or humor.

A concrete noun is something that can be experienced through the senses (touch, taste, hear, smell, see). Examples of concrete nouns are birds, skateboard, pie, and car.

A collective noun refers to a collection of people, places, or things that act as one. Examples of collective nouns are as follows: team, class, jury, family, audience, and flock.

Pronouns

A word used in place of a noun is known as a *pronoun*. Pronouns are words like *I, mine, hers,* and *us*.

Pronouns can be split into different classifications (see below) which make them easier to learn; however, it's not important to memorize the classifications.

- Personal pronouns: refer to people
- First person: we, I, our, mine
- Second person: you, yours
- Third person: he, them
- Possessive pronouns: demonstrate ownership (mine, my, his, yours)
- Interrogative pronouns: ask questions (what, which, who, whom, whose)
- Relative pronouns: include the five interrogative pronouns and others that are relative (whoever, whomever, that, when, where)
- Demonstrative pronouns: replace something specific (this, that, those, these)
- Reciprocal pronouns: indicate something was done or given in return (each other, one another)
- Indefinite pronouns: have a nonspecific status (anybody, whoever, someone, everybody, somebody)

Indefinite pronouns such as *anybody, whoever, someone, everybody*, and *somebody* command a singular verb form, but others such as *all, none,* and *some* could require a singular or plural verb form.

Antecedents

An *antecedent* is the noun to which a pronoun refers; it needs to be written or spoken before the pronoun is used. For many pronouns, antecedents are imperative for clarity. In particular, many of the personal, possessive, and demonstrative pronouns need antecedents. Otherwise, it would be unclear who or what someone is referring to when they use a pronoun like *he* or *this*.

Pronoun reference means that the pronoun should refer clearly to one, clear, unmistakable noun (the antecedent).

Pronoun-antecedent agreement refers to the need for the antecedent and the corresponding pronoun to agree in gender, person, and number. Here are some examples:

> The *kidneys* (plural antecedent) are part of the urinary system. *They* (plural pronoun) serve several roles."
>
> The kidneys are part of the *urinary system* (singular antecedent). *It* (singular pronoun) is also known as the renal system.

Pronoun Cases

The subjective pronouns —*I, you, he/she/it, we, they,* and *who*—are the subjects of the sentence.

> Example: *They* have a new house.

The objective pronouns—*me, you* (*singular*), *him/her, us, them,* and *whom*—are used when something is being done for or given to someone; they are objects of the action.

> Example: The teacher has an apple for *us*.

The possessive pronouns—*mine, my, your, yours, his, hers, its, their, theirs, our,* and *ours*—are used to denote that something (or someone) belongs to someone (or something).

Example: It's *their* chocolate cake.
Even Better Example: It's *my* chocolate cake!

One of the greatest challenges and worst abuses of pronouns concerns *who* and *whom*. Just knowing the following rule can eliminate confusion. *Who* is a subjective-case pronoun used only as a subject or subject complement. *Whom* is only objective-case and, therefore, the object of the verb or preposition.

Who is going to the concert?

You are going to the concert with *whom*?

Hint: When using *who* or *whom*, think of whether someone would say *he* or *him*. If the answer is *he*, use *who*. If the answer is *him*, use *whom*. This trick is easy to remember because *he* and *who* both end in vowels, and *him* and *whom* both end in the letter *M*.

Verbs

The *verb* is the part of speech that describes an action, state of being, or occurrence.

A *verb* forms the main part of a predicate of a sentence. This means that the verb explains what the noun (which will be discussed shortly) is doing. A simple example is *time flies*. The verb *flies* explains what the action of the noun, *time*, is doing. This example is a *main* verb.

Helping (*auxiliary*) verbs are words like *have, do, be, can, may, should, must,* and *will.* "I *should* go to the store." Helping verbs assist main verbs in expressing tense, ability, possibility, permission, or obligation.

Particles are minor function words like *not, in, out, up,* or *down* that become part of the verb itself. "I might *not*."

Participles are words formed from verbs that are often used to modify a noun, noun phrase, verb, or verb phrase.

The *running* teenager collided with the cyclist.

Participles can also create compound verb forms.

He is *speaking*.

Verbs have five basic forms: the *base* form, the *-s* form, the *-ing* form, the *past* form, and the *past participle* form.

The *past* forms are either *regular* (*love/loved; hate/hated*) or *irregular* because they don't end by adding the common past tense suffix "-ed" (*go/went; fall/fell; set/set*).

Verb Forms

Shifting verb forms entails *conjugation*, which is used to indicate *tense, voice,* or *mood*.

Verb tense is used to show when the action in the sentence took place. There are several different verb tenses, and it is important to know how and when to use them. Some verb tenses can be achieved by changing the form of the verb, while others require the use of helping verbs (e.g., *is, was,* or *has*).

Present tense shows the action is happening currently or is ongoing:

I walk to work every morning.

She is stressed about the deadline.

Past tense shows that the action happened in the past or that the state of being is in the past:

I walked to work yesterday morning.

She was stressed about the deadline.

Future tense shows that the action will happen in the future or is a future state of being:

I will walk to work tomorrow morning.

She will be stressed about the deadline.

Present perfect tense shows action that began in the past, but continues into the present:

I have walked to work all week.

She has been stressed about the deadline.

Past perfect tense shows an action was finished before another took place:

I had walked all week until I sprained my ankle.

She had been stressed about the deadline until we talked about it.

Future perfect tense shows an action that will be completed at some point in the future:

By the time the bus arrives, I will have walked to work already.

<u>Voice</u>

Verbs can be in the active or passive voice. When the subject completes the action, the verb is in *active voice*. When the subject receives the action of the sentence, the verb is in *passive voice*.

Active: Jamie ate the ice cream.

Passive: The ice cream was eaten by Jamie.

In active voice, the subject (*Jamie*) is the "do-er" of the action (*ate*). In passive voice, the subject *ice cream* receives the action of being eaten.

While passive voice can add variety to writing, active voice is the generally preferred sentence structure.

<u>Mood</u>

Mood is used to show the speaker's feelings about the subject matter. In English, there is *indicative mood, imperative mood,* and *subjective mood.*

Indicative mood is used to state facts, ask questions, or state opinions:

Bob will make the trip next week.

When can Bob make the trip?

Imperative mood is used to state a command or make a request:

Wait in the lobby.

Please call me next week.

Subjunctive mood is used to express a wish, an opinion, or a hope that is contrary to fact:

If I were in charge, none of this would have happened.

Allison wished she could take the exam over again when she saw her score.

Adjectives

Adjectives are words used to modify nouns and pronouns. They can be used alone or in a series and are used to further define or describe the nouns they modify.

Mark made us a delicious, four-course meal.

The words *delicious* and *four-course* are adjectives that describe the kind of meal Mark made.

Articles are also considered adjectives because they help to describe nouns. Articles can be general or specific. The three articles in English are: a, an, and the.

Indefinite articles (a, an) are used to refer to nonspecific nouns. The article *a* proceeds words beginning with consonant sounds, and the article *an* proceeds words beginning with vowel sounds.

A car drove by our house.

An alligator was loose at the zoo.

He has always wanted a ukulele. (The first *u* makes a *y* sound.)

Note that *a* and *an* should only proceed nonspecific nouns that are also singular. If a nonspecific noun is plural, it does not need a preceding article.

Alligators were loose at the zoo.

The *definite article (the)* is used to refer to specific nouns:

The car pulled into our driveway.

Note that *the* should proceed all specific nouns regardless of whether they are singular or plural.

The cars pulled into our driveway.

Comparative adjectives are used to compare nouns. When they are used in this way, they take on positive, comparative, or superlative form.

The *positive* form is the normal form of the adjective:

Alicia is tall.

The *comparative* form shows a comparison between two things:

Alicia is taller than Maria.

Superlative form shows comparison between more than two things:

Alicia is the tallest girl in her class.

Usually, the comparative and superlative can be made by adding *–er* and *–est* to the positive form, but some verbs call for the helping verbs *more* or *most*. Other exceptions to the rule include adjectives like *bad*, which uses the comparative *worse* and the superlative *worst*.

An adjective phrase is not a bunch of adjectives strung together, but a group of words that describes a noun or pronoun and, thus, functions as an adjective. *Very ugly* is an adjective phrase; so are *way too fat* and *faster than a speeding bullet.*

Adverbs

Adverbs have more functions than adjectives because they modify or qualify verbs, adjectives, or other adverbs as well as word groups that express a relation of place, time, circumstance, or cause. Therefore, adverbs answer any of the following questions: *How, when, where, why, in what way, how often, how much, in what condition,* and/or *to what degree. How good looking is he? He is* <u>*very*</u> *handsome.*

Here are some examples of adverbs for different situations:

- how: quickly
- when: daily
- where: there
- in what way: easily
- how often: often
- how much: much
- in what condition: badly
- what degree: hardly

As one can see, for some reason, many adverbs end in *-ly.*

Adverbs do things like emphasize (*really, simply,* and *so*), amplify (*heartily, completely,* and *positively*), and tone down (*almost, somewhat,* and *mildly*).

Adverbs also come in phrases.

The dog ran as <u>*though his life depended on it.*</u>

Prepositions

Prepositions are connecting words and, while there are only about 150 of them, they are used more often than any other individual groups of words. They describe relationships between other words. They are placed before a noun or pronoun, forming a phrase that modifies another word in the sentence.

Prepositional phrases begin with a preposition and end with a noun or pronoun, the *object of the preposition. A pristine lake is* *near the store* *and* *behind the bank.*

Some commonly used prepositions are *about, after, anti, around, as, at, behind, beside, by, for, from, in, into, of, off, on, to,* and *with.*

Complex prepositions, which also come before a noun or pronoun, consist of two or three words such as *according to, in regards to,* and *because of.*

Conjunctions

Conjunctions are vital words that connect words, phrases, thoughts, and ideas. Conjunctions show relationships between components. There are two types:

Coordinating conjunctions are the primary class of conjunctions placed between words, phrases, clauses, and sentences that are of equal grammatical rank; the coordinating conjunctions are for, and, nor, but, or, yes, and so. A useful memorization trick is to remember that all the first letters of these conjunctions collectively spell the word *fanboys*.

> I need to go shopping, *but* I must be careful to leave enough money in the bank.
> She wore a black, red, *and* white shirt.

Subordinating conjunctions are the secondary class of conjunctions. They connect two unequal parts, one *main* (or *independent*) and the other *subordinate* (or *dependent*). I must go to the store *even though* I do not have enough money in the bank.

> *Because* I read the review, I do not want to go to the movie.

Notice that the presence of subordinating conjunctions makes clauses dependent. *I read the review* is an independent clause, but *because* makes the clause dependent. Thus, it needs an independent clause to complete the sentence.

Interjections

Interjections are words used to express emotion. Examples include *wow*, *ouch*, and *hooray*. Interjections are often separate from sentences; in those cases, the interjection is directly followed by an exclamation point. In other cases, the interjection is included in a sentence and followed by a comma. The punctuation plays a big role in the intensity of the emotion that the interjection is expressing. Using a comma or semicolon indicates less excitement than using an exclamation mark.

Capitalization Rules

Here's a non-exhaustive list of things that should be capitalized.

- The first word of every sentence
- The first word of every line of poetry
- The first letter of proper nouns (World War II)
- Holidays (Valentine's Day)
- The days of the week and months of the year (Tuesday, March)
- The first word, last word, and all major words in the titles of books, movies, songs, and other creative works (In the novel, *To Kill a Mockingbird*, note that *a* is lowercase since it's not a major word, but *to* is capitalized since it's the first word of the title.)
- Titles when preceding a proper noun (President Roberto Gonzales, Aunt Judy)

When simply using a word such as president or secretary, though, the word is not capitalized.

Officers of the new business must include a *president* and *treasurer*.

Seasons—spring, fall, etc.—are not capitalized.

North, *south*, *east*, and *west* are capitalized when referring to regions but are not when being used for directions. In general, if it's preceded by *the* it should be capitalized.

I'm from the South.
I drove south.

End Punctuation

Periods (.) are used to end a sentence that is a statement (*declarative*) or a command (*imperative*). They should not be used in a sentence that asks a question or is an exclamation. Periods are also used in abbreviations, which are shortened versions of words.

- Declarative: The boys refused to go to sleep.
- Imperative: Walk down to the bus stop.
- Abbreviations: Joan Roberts, M.D., Apple Inc., Mrs. Adamson
- If a sentence ends with an abbreviation, it is inappropriate to use two periods. It should end with a single period after the abbreviation.

The chef gathered the ingredients for the pie, which included apples, flour, sugar, etc.

Question marks (?) are used with direct questions (*interrogative*). An *indirect question* can use a period:

Interrogative: When does the next bus arrive?

Indirect Question: I wonder when the next bus arrives.

An *exclamation point (!)* is used to show strong emotion or can be used as an *interjection*. This punctuation should be used sparingly in formal writing situations.

What an amazing shot!

Whoa!

Commas

A *comma* (,) is the punctuation mark that signifies a pause—breath—between parts of a sentence. It denotes a break of flow. Proper comma usage helps readers understand the writer's intended emphasis of ideas.

In a complex sentence—one that contains a subordinate (dependent) clause or clauses—the use of a comma is dictated by where the subordinate clause is located. If the subordinate clause is located before the main clause, a comma is needed between the two clauses.

I will not pay for the steak, *because I don't have that much money*.

Generally, if the subordinate clause is placed after the main clause, no punctuation is needed. I did well on my exam because I studied two hours the night before. Notice how the last clause is dependent because it requires the earlier independent clauses to make sense.

Use a comma on both sides of an interrupting phrase.

I will pay for the ice cream, chocolate and vanilla, and then will eat it all myself.

The words forming the phrase in italics are nonessential (extra) information. To determine if a phrase is nonessential, try reading the sentence without the phrase and see if it's still coherent.

A comma is not necessary in this next sentence because no interruption—nonessential or extra information—has occurred. Read sentences aloud when uncertain.

I will pay for his chocolate and vanilla ice cream and then will eat it all myself.

If the nonessential phrase comes at the beginning of a sentence, a comma should only go at the end of the phrase. If the phrase comes at the end of a sentence, a comma should only go at the beginning of the phrase.

Other types of interruptions include the following:

- interjections: Oh no, I am not going.
- abbreviations: Barry Potter, M.D., specializes in heart disorders.
- direct addresses: Yes, Claudia, I am tired and going to bed.
- parenthetical phrases: His wife, lovely as she was, was not helpful.
- transitional phrases: Also, it is not possible.

The second comma in the following sentence is called an Oxford comma.

I will pay for ice cream, syrup, and pop.

It is a comma used after the second-to-last item in a series of three or more items. It comes before the word *or* or *and*. Not everyone uses the Oxford comma; it is optional, but many believe it is needed. The comma functions as a tool to reduce confusion in writing. So, if omitting the Oxford comma would cause confusion, then it's best to include it.

Commas are used in math to mark the place of thousands in numerals, breaking them up so they are easier to read. Other uses for commas are in dates (*March 19, 2016*), letter greetings (*Dear Sally,*), and in between cities and states (*Louisville, KY*).

Semicolons

A *semicolon (;)* is used to connect ideas in a sentence in some way. There are three main ways to use semicolons.

Link two independent clauses without the use of a coordinating conjunction:

I was late for work again; I'm definitely going to get fired.

Link two independent clauses with a transitional word:

> The songs were all easy to play; therefore, he didn't need to spend too much time practicing.

Between items in a series that are already separated by commas or if necessary to separate lengthy items in a list:

> Starbucks has locations in Media, PA; Swarthmore, PA; and Morton, PA.

> Several classroom management issues presented in the study: the advent of a poor teacher persona in the context of voice, dress, and style; teacher follow-through from the beginning of the school year to the end; and the depth of administrative support, including ISS and OSS protocol.

Colons

A *colon* is used after an independent clause to present an explanation or draw attention to what comes next in the sentence. There are several uses.

Explanations of ideas:

> They soon learned the hardest part about having a new baby: sleep deprivation.

Lists of items:

> Shari picked up all the supplies she would need for the party: cups, plates, napkins, balloons, streamers, and party favors.

Time, subtitles, general salutations:

> The time is 7:15.

> I read a book entitled *Pluto: A Planet No More*.

> To whom it may concern:

Parentheses and Dashes

Parentheses are half-round brackets that look like this: *( )*. They set off a word, phrase, or sentence that is an afterthought, explanation, or side note relevant to the surrounding text but not essential. A pair of commas is often used to set off this sort of information, but parentheses are generally used for information that would not fit well within a sentence or that the writer deems not important enough to be structurally part of the sentence.

> The picture of the heart (see above) shows the major parts you should memorize.
> Mount Everest is one of three mountains in the world that are over 28,000 feet high (K2 and Kanchenjunga are the other two).

See how the sentences above are complete without the parenthetical statements? In the first example, *see above* would not have fit well within the flow of the sentence. The second parenthetical statement could have been a separate sentence, but the writer deemed the information not pertinent to the topic.

The dash (—) is a mark longer than a hyphen used as a punctuation mark in sentences and to set apart a relevant thought. Even after plucking out the line separated by the dash marks, the sentence will be intact and make sense.

> Looking out the airplane window at the landmarks—Lake Clarke, Thompson Community College, and the bridge—she couldn't help but feel excited to be home.

The dashes use is similar to that of parentheses or a pair of commas. So, what's the difference? Many believe that using dashes makes the clause within them stand out while using parentheses is subtler. It's advised to not use dashes when commas could be used instead.

Ellipses

An *ellipsis* (...) consists of three handy little dots that can speak volumes on behalf of irrelevant material. Writers use them in place of words, lines, phrases, list content, or paragraphs that might just as easily have been omitted from a passage of writing. This can be done to save space or to focus only on the specifically relevant material.

> Exercise is good for some unexpected reasons. Watkins writes, "Exercise has many benefits such as...reducing cancer risk."

In the example above, the ellipsis takes the place of the other benefits of exercise that are more expected.

The ellipsis may also be used to show a pause in sentence flow.

> "I'm wondering...how this could happen," Dylan said in a soft voice.

Quotation Marks

Double *quotation marks* are used to at the beginning and end of a direct quote. They are also used with certain titles and to indicate that a term being used is slang or referenced in the sentence. Quotation marks should not be used with an indirect quote. Single quotation marks are used to indicate a quote within a quote.

> Direct quote: "The weather is supposed to be beautiful this week," she said.
>
> Indirect quote: One of the customers asked if the sale prices were still in effect.
>
> Quote within a quote: "My little boy just said 'Mama, I want cookie,'" Maria shared.

Titles: Quotation marks should also be used to indicate titles of short works or sections of larger works, such as chapter titles. Other works that use quotation marks include poems, short stories, newspaper articles, magazine articles, web page titles, and songs.

> "The Road Not Taken" is my favorite poem by Robert Frost.
>
> "What a Wonderful World" is one of my favorite songs.

Specific or emphasized terms: Quotation marks can also be used to indicate a technical term or to set off a word that is being discussed in a sentence. Quotation marks can also indicate sarcasm.

> The new step, called "levigation", is a very difficult technique.

> He said he was "hungry" multiple times, but he only ate two bites.

Use with other punctuation: The use of quotation marks with other punctuation varies, depending on the role of the ending or separating punctuation.

In American English, *periods* and *commas* always go inside the quotation marks:

> "This is the last time you are allowed to leave early," his boss stated.

> The newscaster said, "We have some breaking news to report."

Question marks or *exclamation points* go inside the quotation marks when they are part of a direct quote:

> The doctor shouted, "Get the crash cart!"

When the question mark or exclamation point is part of the sentence, not the quote, it should be placed outside of the quotation marks:

> Was it Jackie that said, "Get some potatoes at the store"?

Apostrophes

This punctuation mark, the apostrophe (') is a versatile mark. It has several different functions:

- Quotes: Apostrophes are used when a second quote is needed within a quote.
  - In my letter to my friend, I wrote, "The girl had to get a new purse, and guess what Mary did? She said, 'I'd like to go with you to the store.' I knew Mary would buy it for her."
- Contractions: Another use for an apostrophe in the quote above is a contraction. *I'd is used for I would.*
- Possession: An apostrophe followed by the letter s shows possession (Mary's purse). If the possessive word is plural, the apostrophe generally just follows the word. Not all possessive pronouns require apostrophes.
  - The trees' leaves are all over the ground.

Hyphens

The *hyphen* (-) is a small hash mark that can be used to join words to show that they are linked.

Hyphenate two words that work together as a single adjective (a compound adjective).

> honey-covered biscuits

Some words always require hyphens, even if not serving as an adjective.

merry-go-round

Hyphens always go after certain prefixes like *anti-* & *all-*.

Hyphens should also be used when the absence of the hyphen would cause a strange vowel combination (*semi-engineer*) or confusion. For example, *re-collect* should be used to describe something being gathered twice rather than being written as *recollect*, which means to remember.

Subjects

Every sentence must include a subject and a verb. The *subject* of a sentence is who or what the sentence is about. It's often directly stated and can be determined by asking "Who?" or "What?" did the action:

Most sentences contain a direct subject, in which the subject is mentioned in the sentence.

Kelly mowed the lawn.

Who mowed the lawn? *Kelly*

The air-conditioner ran all night

What ran all night? *the air-conditioner*

The subject of imperative sentences is *you*, because imperative subjects are commands. the subject is implied because it is a command:

Go home after the meeting.

Who should go home after the meeting? *you* (implied)

In *expletive sentences* that start with "there are" or "there is," the subject is found after the predicate. The subject cannot be "there," so it must be another word in the sentence:

There is a cup sitting on the coffee table.

What is sitting on the coffee table? *a cup*

Simple and Complete Subjects

A *complete subject* includes the simple subject and all the words modifying it, including articles and adjectives. A *simple subject* is the single noun without its modifiers.

A warm, chocolate-chip cookie sat on the kitchen table.

Complete subject: *a warm, chocolate-chip cookie*

Simple subject: *cookie*

The words *a, warm, chocolate,* and *chip* all modify the simple subject *cookie*.

There might also be a *compound subject*, which would be two or more nouns without the modifiers.

A little girl and her mother walked into the shop.

Complete subject: *A little girl and her mother*

Compound subject: *girl, mother*

In this case, *the girl and her mother* are both completing the action of walking into the shop, so this is a *compound subject*.

Predicates

In addition to the subject, a sentence must also have a predicate. The *predicate* contains a verb and tells something about the subject. In addition to the verb, a predicate can also contain a direct or indirect object, object of a preposition, and other phrases.

The cats napped on the front porch.

In this sentence, *cats* is the subject because the sentence is about cats.

The *complete predicate* is everything else in the sentence: *napped on the front porch.* This phrase is the predicate because it tells us what the cats did.

This sentence can be broken down into a simple subject and predicate:

Cats napped.

In this sentence, *cats* is the simple subject, and *napped* is the *simple predicate*.

Although the sentence is very short and doesn't offer much information, it's still considered a complete sentence because it contains a subject and predicate.

Like a compound subject, a sentence can also have a ***compound predicate***. This is when the subject is or does two or more things in the sentence.

This easy chair reclines and swivels.

In this sentence, *this easy chair* is the complete subject. *Reclines and swivels* shows two actions of the chair, so this is the compound predicate.

Subject-Verb Agreement

The subject of a sentence and its verb must agree. The cornerstone rule of subject-verb agreement is that subject and verb must agree in number. Whether the subject is singular or plural, the verb must follow suit.

Incorrect: The houses is new.
Correct: The houses are new.
Also Correct: The house is new.

In other words, a singular subject requires a singular verb; a plural subject requires a plural verb.

The words or phrases that come between the subject and verb do not alter this rule.

> Incorrect: The houses built of brick is new.
> Correct: The houses built of brick are new.
>
> Incorrect: The houses with the sturdy porches is new.
> Correct: The houses with the sturdy porches are new.

The subject will always follow the verb when a sentence begins with *here* or *there.* Identify these with care.

> Incorrect: Here *is* the *houses* with sturdy porches.
> Correct: Here *are* the *houses* with sturdy porches.

The subject in the sentences above is not *here*, it is *houses*. Remember, *here* and *there* are never subjects. Be careful that contractions such as *here's* or *there're* do not cause confusion!

Two subjects joined by *and* require a plural verb form, except when the two combine to make one thing:

> Incorrect: Garrett and Jonathan is over there.
> Correct: Garrett and Jonathan are over there.
>
> Incorrect: Spaghetti and meatballs are a delicious meal!
> Correct: Spaghetti and meatballs is a delicious meal!

In the example above, *spaghetti and meatballs* is a compound noun. However, *Garrett and Jonathan* is not a compound noun.

Two singular subjects joined by *or, either/or,* or *neither/nor* call for a singular verb form.

> Incorrect: Butter or syrup are acceptable.
> Correct: Butter or syrup is acceptable.

Plural subjects joined by *or*, *either/or*, or *neither/nor* are, indeed, plural.

> The chairs or the boxes are being moved next.

If one subject is singular and the other is plural, the verb should agree with the closest noun.

> Correct: The chair or the boxes are being moved next.
> Correct: The chairs or the box is being moved next.

Some plurals of money, distance, and time call for a singular verb.

> Incorrect: Three dollars *are* enough to buy that.
> Correct: Three dollars *is* enough to buy that.

For words declaring degrees of quantity such as *many of, some of,* or *most of,* let the noun that follows *of* be the guide:

Incorrect: Many of the books is in the shelf.
Correct: Many of the books are in the shelf.

Incorrect: Most of the pie *are* on the table.
Correct: Most of the pie *is* on the table.

For indefinite pronouns like anybody or everybody, use singular verbs.

Everybody *is* going to the store.

However, the pronouns *few, many, several, all, some,* and *both* have their own rules and use plural forms.

Some *are* ready.

Some nouns like *crowd* and *congress* are called *collective nouns* and they require a singular verb form.

Congress *is* in session.
The news *is* over.

Books and movie titles, though, including plural nouns such as *Great Expectations*, also require a singular verb. Remember that only the subject affects the verb. While writing tricky subject-verb arrangements, say them aloud. Listen to them. Once the rules have been learned, one's ear will become sensitive to them, making it easier to pick out what's right and what's wrong.

Direct Objects

The *direct object* is the part of the sentence that receives the action of the verb. It is a noun and can usually be found after the verb. To find the direct object, first find the verb, and then ask the question *who* or *what* after it.

The bear climbed the tree.

What did the bear climb? *the tree*

Indirect Objects

An *indirect object* receives the direct object. It is usually found between the verb and the direct object. A strategy for identifying the indirect object is to find the verb and ask the questions *to whom/for whom* or *to what/ for what.*

Jane made her daughter a cake.

For whom did Jane make the cake? *her daughter*

Cake is the direct object because it is what Jane made, and *daughter* is the indirect object because she receives the cake.

Complements

A *complement* completes the meaning of an expression. A complement can be a pronoun, noun, or adjective. A verb complement refers to the direct object or indirect object in the sentence. An object complement gives more information about the direct object:

> The magician got the kids excited.
>
> *Kids* is the direct object, and *excited* is the object complement.

A *subject complement* comes after a linking verb. It is typically an adjective or noun that gives more information about the subject:

> The king was noble and spared the thief's life.

Noble describes the *king* and follows the linking verb *was*.

Predicate Nouns

A *predicate noun* renames the subject:

> John is a carpenter.

The subject is *John*, and the predicate noun is *carpenter*.

Predicate Adjectives

A *predicate adjective* describes the subject:

> Margaret is beautiful.

The subject is *Margaret*, and the predicate adjective is *beautiful*.

Homonyms

Homonyms are words that sound the same but are spelled differently, and they have different meanings. There are several common homonyms that give writers trouble.

<u>*There, They're,* and *Their*</u>

The word *there* can be used as an adverb, adjective, or pronoun:

> *There* are ten children on the swim team this summer.
>
> I put my book over *there*, but now I can't find it.

The word *they're* is a contraction of the words *they* and *are*:

> *They're* flying in from Texas on Tuesday.

The word *their* is a possessive pronoun:

> I store *their* winter clothes in the attic.

Its and *It's*

Its is a possessive pronoun:

> The cat licked *its* injured paw.

It's is the contraction for the words *it* and *is*:

> *It's* unbelievable how many people opted not to vote in the last election.

Your and You're

Your is a possessive pronoun:

> Can I borrow *your* lawnmower this weekend?

You're is a contraction for the words *you* and *are*:

> *You're* about to embark on a fantastic journey.

To, Too, and *Two*

To is an adverb or a preposition used to show direction, relationship, or purpose:

> We are going *to* New York.
>
> They are going *to* see a show.

Too is an adverb that means more than enough, also, and very:

> You have had *too* much candy.
>
> We are on vacation that week, *too*.

Two is the written-out form of the numeral 2:

> *Two* of the shirts didn't fit, so I will have to return them.

New and *Knew*

New is an adjective that means recent:

> There's a *new* customer on the phone.

Knew is the past tense of the verb *know*:

> I *knew* you'd have fun on this ride.

Affect and *Effect*

Affect and *effect* are complicated because they are used as both nouns and verbs, have similar meanings, and are pronounced the same.

	Affect	**Effect**
Noun Definition	emotional state	result
Noun Example	The patient's affect was flat.	The effects of smoking are well documented.
Verb Definition	to influence	to bring about
Verb Example	The pollen count affects my allergies.	The new candidate hopes to effect change.

Independent and Dependent Clauses

Independent and *dependent* clauses are strings of words that contain both a subject and a verb. An independent clause *can* stand alone as complete thought, but a dependent clause *cannot*. A dependent clause relies on other words to be a complete sentence.

Independent clause: The keys are on the counter.
Dependent clause: If the keys are on the counter

Notice that both clauses have a subject (*keys*) and a verb (*are*). The independent clause expresses a complete thought, but the word *if* at the beginning of the dependent clause makes it *dependent* on other words to be a complete thought.

Independent clause: If the keys are on the counter, please give them to me.

This presents a complete sentence since it includes at least one verb and one subject and is a complete thought. In this case, the independent clause has two subjects (*keys* & an implied *you*) and two verbs (*are* & *give*).

Independent clause: I went to the store.
Dependent clause: Because we are out of milk,

Complete Sentence: Because we are out of milk, I went to the store.
Complete Sentence: I went to the store because we are out of milk.

Phrases

A *phrase* is a group of words that do not make a complete thought or a clause. They are parts of sentences or clauses. Phrases can be used as nouns, adjectives, or adverbs. A phrase does not contain both a subject and a verb.

Prepositional Phrases

A *prepositional phrase* shows the relationship between a word in the sentence and the object of the preposition. The object of the preposition is a noun that follows the preposition.

The orange pillows are on the couch.

On is the preposition, and *couch* is the object of the preposition.

She brought her friend with the nice car.

With is the preposition, and *car* is the object of the preposition. Here are some common prepositions:

about	as	at	after
by	for	from	in
of	on	to	with

<u>Verbals and Verbal Phrases</u>

Verbals are forms of verbs that act as other parts of speech. They can be used as nouns, adjectives, or adverbs. Though they are use verb forms, they are not to be used as the verb in the sentence. A word group that is based on a verbal is considered a *verbal phrase*. There are three major types of verbals: *participles, gerunds,* and *infinitives.*

Participles are verbals that act as adjectives. The present participle ends in *–ing*, and the past participle ends in *–d*, *-ed*, *-n*, or*-t*.

Verb	**Present Participle**	**Past Participle**
walk	walking	walked
share	sharing	shared

Participial phrases are made up of the participle and modifiers, complements, or objects.

Crying for most of an hour, the baby didn't seem to want to nap.

Having already taken this course, the student was bored during class.

Crying for most of an hour and *Having already taken this course* are the participial phrases.

Gerunds are verbals that are used as nouns and end in *–ing*. A gerund can be the subject or object of the sentence like a noun. Note that a present participle can also end in *–ing*, so it is important to distinguish between the two. The gerund is used as a noun, while the participle is used as an adjective.

Swimming is my favorite sport.

I wish I were sleeping.

A *gerund phrase* includes the gerund and any modifiers or complements, direct objects, indirect objects, or pronouns.

Cleaning the house is my least favorite weekend activity.

Cleaning the house is the gerund phrase acting as the subject of the sentence.

The most important goal this year is raising money for charity.

Raising money for charity is the gerund phrase acting as the direct object.

The police accused the woman of stealing the car.

The *gerund* phrase *stealing the car* is the object of the preposition in this sentence.

An *infinitive* is a verbal made up of the word to and a verb. Infinitives can be used as nouns, adjectives, or adverbs.

Examples: To eat, to jump, to swim, to lie, to call, to work

An *infinitive phrase* is made up of the infinitive plus any complements or modifiers. The infinitive phrase *to wait* is used as the subject in this sentence:

To wait was not what I had in mind.

The infinitive phrase *to sing* is used as the subject complement in this sentence:

Her dream is to sing.

The infinitive phrase *to grow* is used as an adverb in this sentence:

Children must eat to grow.

Appositive Phrases

An *appositive* is a noun or noun phrase that renames a noun that comes immediately before it in the sentence. An appositive can be a single word or several words. These phrases can be *essential* or *nonessential*. An essential appositive phrase is necessary to the meaning of the sentence and a nonessential appositive phrase is not. It is important to be able to distinguish these for purposes of comma use.

Essential: My sister Christina works at a school.

Naming which sister is essential to the meaning of the sentence, so no commas are needed.

Nonessential: My sister, who is a teacher, is coming over for dinner tonight.

Who is a teacher is not essential to the meaning of the sentence, so commas are required.

Absolute Phrases

An *absolute phrase* modifies a noun without using a conjunction. It is not the subject of the sentence and is not a complete thought on its own. Absolute phrases are set off from the independent clause with a comma.

Arms outstretched, she yelled at the sky.

All things considered, this has been a great day.

The Four Types of Sentence Structures

A *simple sentence* has one independent clause.

I am going to win.

A *compound sentence* has two independent clauses. A conjunction—*for, and, nor, but, or, yet, so*—links them together. Note that each of the independent clauses has a subject and a verb.

I am going to win, but the odds are against me.

A *complex sentence* has one independent clause and one or more dependent clauses.

I am going to win, even though I don't deserve it.

Even though I don't deserve it is a dependent clause. It does not stand on its own. Some conjunctions that link an independent and a dependent clause are *although*, *because*, *before*, *after*, *that*, *when*, *which*, and *while*.

A *compound-complex sentence* has at least three clauses, two of which are independent and at least one that is a dependent clause.

While trying to dance, I tripped over my partner's feet, but I regained my balance quickly.

The dependent clause is *While trying to dance*.

Sentence Fragments

A *sentence fragment* is an incomplete sentence. An independent clause is made up of a subject and a predicate, and both are needed to make a complete sentence.

Sentence fragments often begin with *relative pronouns* (when, which*), subordinating conjunctions (*because, although*)* or *gerunds* (trying, being, seeing). They might be missing the subject or the predicate.

The most common type of fragment is the isolated dependent clause, which can be corrected by joining it to the independent clause that appears before or after the fragment:

Fragment: While the cookies baked.

Correction: While the cookies baked, we played cards. (We played cards while the cookies baked.)

Run-on Sentences

A *run-on sentence* is created when two independent clauses (complete thoughts) are joined without correct punctuation or a conjunction. Run-on sentences can be corrected in the following ways:

- Join the independent clauses with a comma and coordinating conjunction.

  Run-on: We forgot to return the library books we had to pay a fine.

  Correction: We forgot to return the library books, so we had to pay a fine.

- Join the independent clauses with a semicolon, dash, or colon when the clauses are closely related in meaning.

  Run-on: I had a salad for lunch every day this week I feel healthier already.

  Correction: I had a salad for lunch every day this week; I feel healthier already.

- Join the independent clauses with a *semicolon and a conjunctive adverb.*

  Run-on: We arrived at the animal shelter on time however the dog had already been adopted.

  Correction: We arrived at the animal shelter on time; however, the dog had already been adopted.

- Separate the independent clauses into two sentences *with a period.*

  Run-on: He tapes his favorite television show he never misses an episode.

  Correction: He tapes his favorite television show. He never misses an episode.

- *Rearrange the wording* of the sentence to create an independent clause and a dependent clause.

  Run-on: My wedding date is coming up I am getting more excited to walk down the aisle.

  Correction: As my wedding date approaches, I am getting more excited to walk down the aisle.

Dangling and Misplaced Modifiers

A *modifier* is a phrase that describes, alters, limits, or gives more information about a word in the sentence. The two most common issues are dangling and misplaced modifiers.

A *dangling modifier* is created when the phrase modifies a word that is not clearly stated in the sentence.

> Dangling modifier: Having finished dinner, the dishes were cleared from the table.
>
> Correction: Having finished dinner, Amy cleared the dishes from the table.

In the first sentence, *having finished dinner* appears to modify *the dishes*, which obviously can't finish dinner. The second sentence adds the subject *Amy*, to make it clear who has finished dinner.

> Dangling modifier: Hoping to improve test scores, all new books were ordered for the school.
>
> Correction: Hoping to improve test scores, administrators ordered all new books for the school.
>
> Without the subject *administrators*, it appears the books are hoping to improve test scores, which doesn't make sense.

Misplaced modifiers are placed incorrectly in the sentence, which can cause confusion. Compare these examples:

> Misplaced modifier: Rory purchased a new flat screen television and placed it on the wall above the fireplace, with all the bells and whistles.
>
> Revised: Rory purchased a new flat screen television, with all the bells and whistles, and placed it on the wall above the fireplace.

The bells and whistles should modify the television, not the fireplace.

> Misplaced modifier: The delivery driver arrived late with the pizza, who was usually on time.
>
> Revised: The delivery driver, who usually was on time, arrived late with the pizza.

This suggests that the delivery driver was usually on time, instead of the pizza.

> Misplaced modifier: We saw a family of ducks on the way to church.
>
> Revised: On the way to church, we saw a family of ducks.
>
> The misplaced modifier, here, suggests the *ducks* were on their way to church, instead of the pronoun *we*.

Split Infinitives

An infinitive is made up of the word *to* and a verb, such as: to run, to jump, to ask. A *split infinitive* is created when a word comes between *to* and the verb.

> Split infinitive: To quickly run
>
> Correction: To run quickly
>
> Split infinitive: To quietly ask
>
> Correction: To ask quietly

Double Negatives

A *double negative* is a negative statement that includes two negative elements. This is incorrect in Standard English.

> Incorrect: She hasn't never come to my house to visit.
>
> Correct: She has never come to my house to visit.

The intended meaning is that she has never come to the house, so the double negative is incorrect. However, it is possible to use two negatives to create a positive statement.

> Correct: She was not unhappy with her performance on the quiz.

In this case, the double negative*, was not unhappy*, is intended to show a positive, so it is correct. This means that she was somewhat happy with her performance.

Faulty Parallelism

It is necessary to use parallel construction in sentences that have multiple similar ideas. Using parallel structure provides clarity in writing. *Faulty parallelism* is created when multiple ideas are joined using different sentence structures. Compare these examples:

> Incorrect: We start each practice with stretches, a run, and fielding grounders.
> Correct: We start each practice with stretching, running, and fielding grounders.
>
> Incorrect: I watched some television, reading my book, and fell asleep.
> Correct: I watched some television, read my book, and fell asleep.
>
> Incorrect: *Some of the readiness skills for Kindergarten are to cut with scissors, to tie shoes, and dressing independently.*
> Correct: *Some of the readiness skills for Kindergarten are being able to cut with scissors, to tie shoes, and to dress independently.*

Subordination

If multiple pieces of information in a sentence are not equal, they can be joined by creating an independent clause and a dependent clause. The less important information becomes the *subordinate clause*:

> Draft: The hotel was acceptable. We wouldn't stay at the hotel again.
>
> Revised: Though the hotel was acceptable, we wouldn't stay there again.

The more important information (*we wouldn't stay there again*) becomes the main clause, and the less important information (*the hotel was acceptable*) becomes the subordinate clause.

Practice Questions

Careers

Focus: Students must make revising and editing decisions on the context of a passage on a career-related topic.

Aircraft Engineers

The knowledge of an aircraft engineer is acquired through years of education, and special licenses are required. Ideally, an individual will begin his or her preparation for the profession in high school by taking chemistry, physics, trigonometry, and calculus. Such curricula will aid in one's pursuit of a bachelor's degree in aircraft engineering, which requires several physical and life sciences, mathematics, and design courses.

(2) Some of universities provide internship or apprentice opportunities for the students enrolled in aircraft engineer programs. A bachelor's in aircraft engineering is commonly accompanied by a master's degree in advanced engineering or business administration. Such advanced degrees enable an individual to position himself or herself for executive, faculty, and/or research opportunities. (3) These advanced offices oftentimes require a Professional Engineering (PE) license which can be obtained through additional college courses, professional experience, and acceptable scores on the Fundamentals of Engineering (FE) and Professional Engineering (PE) standardized assessments.

Once the job begins, this line of work requires critical thinking, business skills, problem solving, and creativity. This level of (5) expertise (6) allows aircraft engineers to apply mathematical equations and scientific processes to aeronautical and aerospace issues or inventions. (8) For example, aircraft engineers may test, design, and construct flying vessels such as airplanes, space shuttles, and missile weapons. As a result, aircraft engineers are compensated with generous salaries. In fact, in May 2014, the lowest 10 percent of all American aircraft engineers earned less than $60,110 while the highest paid ten-percent of all American aircraft engineers earned $155,240. (9) In May 2015, the United States Bureau of Labor Statistics (BLS) reported that the median annual salary of aircraft engineers was $107, 830. (10) Conversely, (11) employment opportunities for aircraft engineers are projected to decrease by 2 percent by 2024. This decrease may be the result of a decline in the manufacturing industry. Nevertheless, aircraft engineers who know how to utilize modeling and simulation programs, fluid dynamic software, and robotic engineering tools are projected to remain the most employable.

2015 Annual Salary of Aerospace Engineers

Source: Bureau of Labor Statistics

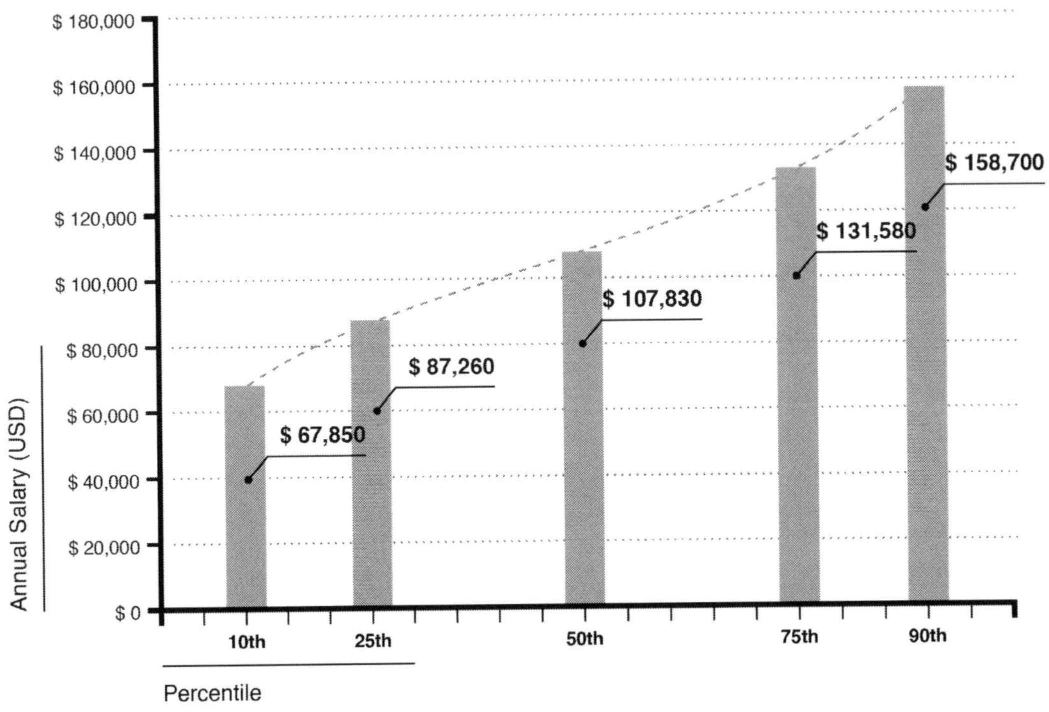

1. What type of text is utilized in the passage?
    a. Argumentative
    b. Narrative
    c. Biographical
    d. Informative

2.
    a. NO CHANGE
    b. Some of universities provided internship or apprentice opportunities
    c. Some of universities provide internship or apprenticeship opportunities
    d. Some universities provide internship or apprenticeship opportunities

3.

a. NO CHANGE

b. These advanced positions oftentimes require acceptable scores on the Fundamentals of Engineering (FE) and Professional Engineering (PE) standardized assessments in order to achieve a Professional Engineering (PE) license. Additional college courses and professional experience help.

c. These advanced offices oftentimes require acceptable scores on the Fundamentals of Engineering (FE) and Professional Engineering (PE) standardized assessments to gain the Professional Engineering (PE) license which can be obtained through additional college courses, professional experience.

d. These advanced positions oftentimes require a Professional Engineering (PE) license which is obtained by acceptable scores on the Fundamentals of Engineering (FE) and Professional Engineering (PE) standardized assessments. Further education and professional experience can help prepare for the assessments.

4. "The knowledge of an aircraft engineer is acquired through years of education." Which statement serves to support this claim?

a. Aircraft engineers are compensated with generous salaries.

b. Such advanced degrees enable an individual to position himself or herself for executive, faculty, or research opportunities.

c. Ideally, an individual will begin his or her preparation for the profession in high school by taking chemistry, physics, trigonometry, and calculus.

d. Aircraft engineers who know how to utilize modeling and simulation programs, fluid dynamic software, and robotic engineering tools will be the most employable.

5. What is the meaning of "expertise" in the marked sentence?

a. Care

b. Skill

c. Work

d. Composition

6.

a. NO CHANGE

b. Inhibits

c. Requires

d. Should

7. In the third paragraph, which of the following claims is supported?

a. This line of work requires critical thinking, business skills, problem solving, and creativity.

b. Aircraft engineers are compensated with generous salaries.

c. The knowledge of an aircraft engineer is acquired through years of education.

d. Those who work hard are rewarded accordingly.

8.

a. NO CHANGE

b. Therefore,

c. However,

d. Furthermore,

9.

a. NO CHANGE

b. May of 2015, the United States Bureau of Labor Statistics (BLS) reported that the median annual salary of aircraft engineers was $107, 830.

c. In May of 2015 the United States Bureau of Labor Statistics (BLS) reported that the median annual salary of aircraft engineers was $107, 830.

d. In May, 2015, the United States Bureau of Labor Statistics (BLS) reported that the median annual salary of aircraft engineers was $107, 830.

10.

a. NO CHANGE

b. Similarly,

c. In other words,

d. Accordingly,

11.

a. NO CHANGE

b. Employment opportunities for aircraft engineers will be projected to decrease by 2 percent in 2024.

c. Employment opportunities for aircraft engineers is projected to decrease by 2 percent in 2024.

d. Employment opportunities for aircraft engineers were projected to decrease by 2 percent in 2024.

History/ Social Studies

Focus: Students must make revising and editing decisions on the context of a passage on a career-related topic.

Attacks of September 11th

On September 11th 2001, a group of terrorists hijacked four American airplanes. The terrorists crashed the planes into the World Trade Center in New York City, the Pentagon in Washington D.C., and a field in Pennsylvania. Nearly 3,000 people died during the attacks, which propelled the United States into a "War on Terror".

About the Terrorists

Terrorists commonly use fear and violence to achieve political goals. The nineteen terrorists who orchestrated and implemented the attacks of September 11th were militants associated with al-Qaeda, an Islamic extremist group founded by Osama bin Landen, Abdullah Azzam, and others in the late 1980s. (13) Bin Laden orchestrated the attacks as a response to what he felt was American injustice against Islam and hatred towards Muslims. In his words, "Terrorism against America deserves to be praised."

Islam is the religion of Muslims, who live mainly in South and Southwest Asia and Sub-Saharan Africa. The majority of Muslims practice Islam peacefully. However, fractures in Islam have led to the growth of Islamic extremists who strictly oppose Western influences. They seek to institute stringent Islamic law and destroy those who (15) violate Islamic code.

In November 2002, bin Laden provided the explicit motives for the 9/11 terror attacks. According to this list, America's support of Israel, military presence in Saudi Arabia, and other anti-Muslim actions were the causes.

The Timeline of the Attacks

The morning of September 11 began like any other for most Americans. Then, at 8:45 a.m., a Boeing 767 plane crashed into the north tower of the World Trade Center in New York City. Hundreds were instantly killed. Others were trapped on higher floors. The (17) crash was initially thought to be a freak accident. When a second plane flew directly into the south tower eighteen minutes later, it was determined that America was under attack.

At 9:45 a.m., a third plane slammed into the Pentagon, America's military headquarters in Washington D.C. The jet fuel of this plane caused a major fire and partial building collapse that resulted in nearly 200 deaths. By 10:00 a.m., the south tower of the World Trade Center collapsed. Thirty minutes later, the north tower followed suit.

While this was happening, a fourth plane that departed from New Jersey, United Flight 93, was hijacked. The passengers learned of the attacks that occurred in New York and Washington D.C. and realized that they faced the same fate as the other planes that crashed. The passengers were determined to overpower the terrorists in an effort to prevent the deaths of additional innocent American citizens. Although the passengers were successful in (18) diverging the plane, it crashed in a western Pennsylvania field and killed everyone on board. The plane's final target remains uncertain, but many believe that United Flight 93 was heading for the White House.

Heroes and Rescuers

Close to 3,000 people died in the World Trade Center attacks. This figure includes 343 New York City firefighters and paramedics, 23 New York City police officers, and 37 Port Authority officers. Nevertheless, thousands of men and women in service worked valiantly to evacuate the buildings, save trapped workers, extinguish infernos, uncover victims trapped in fallen rubble, and tend to nearly 10,000 injured individuals.

About 300 rescue dogs played a major role in the after-attack salvages. Working twelve-hour shifts, the dogs scoured the rubble and alerted paramedics when they found signs of life. While doing so, the dogs served as a source of comfort and therapy for the rescue teams.

Initial Impacts on America

The attacks of September 11, 2001 resulted in the immediate suspension of all air travel. No flights could take off from or land on American soil. American airports and airspace closed to all national and international flights. Therefore, over five hundred flights had to turn back or be redirected to other countries. Canada alone received 226 flights and thousands of stranded passengers. Needless to say, as canceled flights are rescheduled, air travel became backed up and chaotic for quite some time.

At the time of the attacks, George W. Bush was the president of the United States. President Bush announced that "We will make no distinction between the terrorists who committed these acts and those who harbor them." The rate of hate crimes against American Muslims spiked, despite President Bush's call for the country to treat them with respect.

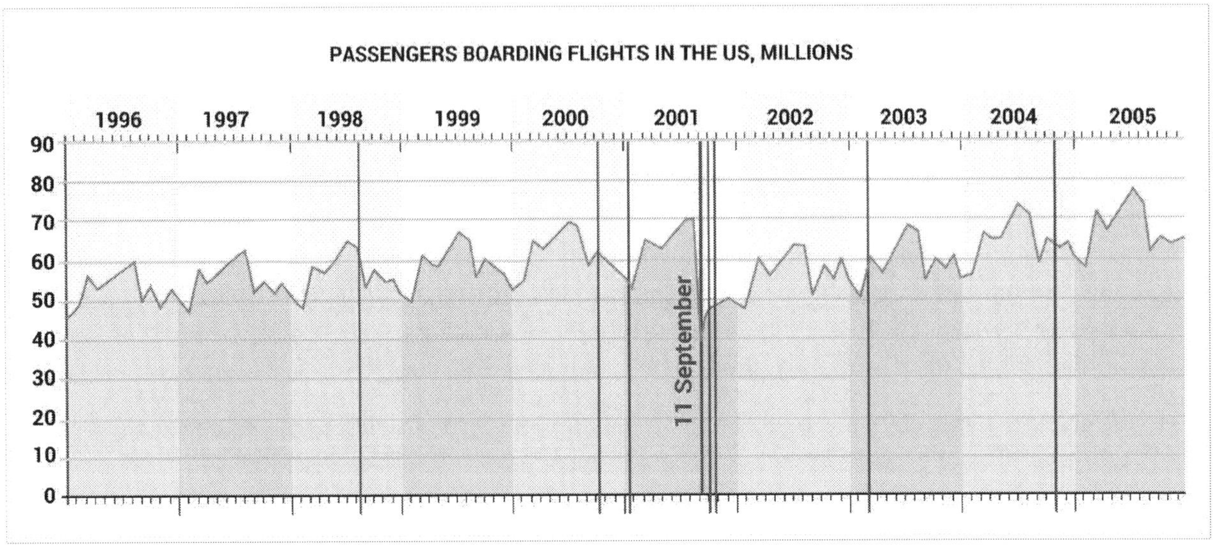

Additionally, relief funds were quickly arranged. The funds were used to support families of the victims, orphaned children, and those with major injuries. In this way, the tragic event brought the citizens together through acts of service towards those directly impacted by the attack.

Long-term Effects of the Attacks

Over the past fifteen years, the attacks of September 11th have transformed the United States' government, travel safety protocols, and international relations. Anti-terrorism legislation became a priority for many countries as law enforcement and intelligence agencies teamed up to find and defeat alleged terrorists.

Present George W. Bush announced a War on Terror. He <u>(21) desired</u> to bring bin Laden and al-Qaeda to justice and prevent future terrorist networks from gaining strength. The War in Afghanistan began in October of 2001 when the United States and British forces bombed al-Qaeda camps. <u>(22) The Taliban, a group of fundamental Muslims who protected Osama bin Laden, was overthrown on December 9, 2001. However, the war continued in order to defeat insurgency campaigns in neighboring countries.</u> Ten years later, the United State Navy SEALS killed Osama bin Laden in Pakistan. During 2014, the United States declared the end of its involvement in the War on Terror in Afghanistan.

Museums and memorials have since been erected to honor and remember the thousands of people who died during the September 11th attacks, including the brave rescue workers who gave their lives in the effort to help others.

12. How does the structure of the text help readers better understand the topic?
  a. By stating that anti-terrorism legislation was a priority for many countries, the reader can determine which laws were made and how they changed the life in the country.
  b. By placing the events in the order that they occurred, readers are better able to understand how the day unfolded.
  c. By using descriptive language, the readers are able to develop detailed images of the events that occurred during September 11, 2001.
  d. None of the above

13.
  a. NO CHANGE
  b. Bin Laden orchestrated the attacks as a response to what he felt was American injustice against Islam, and hatred towards Muslims.
  c. Bin Laden orchestrated the attacks, as a response to what he felt was American injustice against Islam and hatred towards Muslims.
  d. Bin Laden orchestrated the attacks as responding to what he felt was American injustice against Islam and hatred towards Muslims.

14. How could the author best express that most Muslims are peaceful people?
  a. By describing the life of a Muslim after the attacks.
  b. By including an anecdote about a Muslim friend.
  c. By reciting details from religious texts.
  d. By explicitly stating that fact.

15. What word could be used in exchange for "violate"?
  a. Respect
  b. Defile
  c. Deny
  d. Obey

16. What technique does the author use to highlight the impact of United Flight 93?
  a. An image of the crash
  b. An allusion to illustrate what may have occurred had the passengers not taken action
  c. An anecdote about a specific passenger
  d. A point of view consideration, where the author forces the reader to think about how he or she would have responded to such a situation

17. Which of the following would NOT be an appropriate replacement for the underlined portion of the sentence?
  a. First crash was thought to be
  b. Initial crash was thought to be
  c. Thought was that the initial crash
  d. Initial thought was that the crash was

18.
  a. NO CHANGE
  b. Diverting
  c. Converging
  d. Distracting

19. What statement is best supported by the graph included in this passage?
   a. As canceled flights were rescheduled, air travel became backed up and chaotic for quite some time.
   b. Over five hundred flights had to turn back or be redirected to other countries.
   c. Canada alone received 226 flights and thousands of stranded passengers.
   d. The attacks of September 11, 2001 resulted in the immediate suspension of all air travel.

20. What is the purpose of the last paragraph?
   a. It shows that beautiful art can be used to remember a past event.
   b. It demonstrates that Americans will always remember the 9/11 attacks and the lives that were lost.
   c. It explains how America fought back after the attacks.
   d. It provides the author with an opportunity to explain how the location of the towers is used today.

21.
   a. NO CHANGE
   b. Perceived
   c. Intended
   d. Assimilated

22.
   a. NO CHANGE
   b. The Taliban was overthrown on December 9, 2001. They were a group of fundamental Muslims who protected Osama bin Laden. However, the war continued in order to defeat insurgency campaigns in neighboring countries.
   c. The Taliban, a group of fundamental Muslims who protected Osama bin Laden, on December 9, 2001 was overthrown. However, the war continued in order to defeat insurgency campaigns in neighboring countries.
   d. Osama bin Laden's fundamental Muslims who protected him were called the Taliban and overthrown on December 9, 2001. Yet the war continued in order to defeat the insurgency campaigns in neighboring countries.

Humanities

Focus: Students must make revising and editing decisions on the context of a passage on a humanities-related topic.

Fred Hampton

Fred Hampton desired to see lasting social change for African American people through nonviolent means and community recognition. (23) As a result, he became an African American activist during the American Civil Rights Movement and led the Chicago chapter of the Black Panther Party.

Hampton's Education

Hampton was born and raised in Maywood of Chicago, Illinois in 1948. (24) Gifted academically and a natural athlete, he became a stellar baseball player in high school.

After graduating from Proviso East High School in 1966, he later went on to study law at Triton Junior College.

While studying at Triton, Hampton joined and became a leader of the National Association for the Advancement of Colored People (NAACP). (25) As a result of his leadership, the NAACP gained more than 500 members. Hampton worked relentlessly to acquire recreational facilities in the neighborhood and improve the educational resources provided to the impoverished black community of Maywood.

The Black Panthers

The Black Panther Party (BPP) was another activist group that formed around the same time as the NAACP. Hampton was quickly attracted to the Black Panther's approach to the fight for equal rights for African Americans. (26) Hampton eventually joined the chapter and relocated to downtown Chicago to be closer to its headquarters.

His (27) charismatic personality, organizational abilities, sheer determination, and rhetorical skills enabled him to quickly rise through the chapter's ranks. (28) Hampton soon became the leader of the Chicago chapter of the BPP where he organized rallies, taught political education classes, and established a free medical clinic. He also took part in the community police supervision project and played an (40) instrumental role in the BPP breakfast program for impoverished African American children.

Hampton's greatest achievement as the leader of the BPP may be his fight against street gang violence in Chicago. In 1969, Hampton held a press conference where he made the gangs agree to a nonaggression pact known as the Rainbow Coalition. As a result of the pact, a multiracial alliance between blacks, Puerto Ricans, and poor youth was developed.

Assassination

As the Black Panther Party's popularity and influence grew, the Federal Bureau of Investigation (FBI) placed the group under constant surveillance. In an attempt to (30) neutralize the party, the FBI launched several harassment campaigns against the BPP, raided its headquarters in Chicago three times, and arrested over one hundred of the group's members. Hampton was shot during such a raid that occurred on the morning of December 4th, 1969.

In 1976, seven years after the event, it was revealed that William O'Neal, Hampton's trusted bodyguard, was an undercover FBI agent. (31) O'Neal provided the FBI with detailed floor plans of the BPP's headquarters, identifying the exact location of Hampton's bed. It was because of these floor plans that the police were able to target and kill Hampton.

The assassination of Hampton fueled outrage amongst the African American community. It was not until years after the assassination that the police admitted wrongdoing. The Chicago City Council now (32) commemorates December 4th as Fred Hampton Day.

23.

a. NO CHANGE
b. As a result he became an African American activist
c. As a result: he became an African American activist
d. As a result of, he became an African American activist

24. What word could be used in place of the underlined description?

a. Vacuous
b. Energetic
c. Intelligent
d. Athletic

25. Which of the following statements, if true, would further validate the selected sentence?

a. Several of these new members went on to earn scholarships.
b. With this increase in numbers, Hampton was awarded a medal for his contribution to the NAACP.
c. Many of these new members would go on to hold high positions in the organization, often accrediting Hampton for his encouragement and guidance.
d. The NAACP has been growing steadily every year.

26. How else could this sentence be re-structured while maintaining the context of the fourth paragraph?

a. NO CHANGE
b. Eventually, Hampton joined the chapter and relocated to downtown Chicago to be closer to its headquarters.
c. Nevertheless, Hampton joined the chapter and relocated to downtown Chicago to be closer to its headquarters.
d. Hampton then joined the chapter and relocated to downtown Chicago to be closer to its headquarters

27. What word is synonymous with the underlined description?

a. Egotistical
b. Obnoxious
c. Chauvinistic
d. Charming

28.

a. NO CHANGE
b. As the leader of the BPP, Hampton: organized rallies, taught political education classes, and established a free medical clinic.
c. As the leader of the BPP, Hampton; organized rallies, taught political education classes, and established a free medical clinic.
d. As the leader of the BPP, Hampton—organized rallies, taught political education classes, and established a medical free clinic.

29. The author develops the idea that Frank Hampton should not have been killed at the hands of the police. Which could best be used to support that claim?

a. The manner in which the police raided the BPP headquarters.
b. The eventual admission from the police that they were wrong in killing Hampton.
c. The description of previous police raids that resulted in the arrest of hundreds BPP members.
d. All of the above.

30.

a. NO CHANGE
b. Accommodate
c. Assuage
d. Praise

31. How could this sentence be rewritten without losing its original meaning?

a. NO CHANGE
b. O'Neal provided the FBI with detailed floor plans of the BPP's headquarters, which identified the exact location of Hampton's bed.
c. O'Neal provided the FBI with detailed floor plans and Hampton's bed.
d. O'Neal identified the exact location of Hampton's bed that provided the FBI with detailed floor plans of the BPP's headquarters.

32. What word could be used in place of the underlined word?

a. Disregards
b. Memorializes
c. Communicates
d. Denies

33. How would the author likely describe the FBI during the events of the passage?

a. Corrupt
b. Confused
c. Well-intended
d. Prejudiced

Science

Focus: Students must make revising and editing decisions on the context of a passage on a scientific topic.

Here Comes the Flood!

A flood occurs when an area of land that is normally dry becomes submerged with water. Floods have affected Earth since the beginning of time and are caused by many different factors. (36) Flooding can occur slowly or within seconds and can submerge small regions or extend over vast areas of land. Their impact on society and the environment can be harmful or helpful.

What Causes Flooding?

Floods may be caused by natural phenomenon, induced by the activities of humans and other animals, or the failure of an infrastructure. Areas located near bodies of water are prone to flooding as are low-lying regions.

Global warming is the result of air pollution that prevents the sun's radiation from being emitted back into space. Instead, the radiation is trapped in Earth and results in global warming. The warming of the Earth has resulted in climate changes. As a result, floods have been occurring with increasing regularity. Some claim that the increased temperatures on Earth may cause the icebergs to melt. They fear that the melting of icebergs will cause the (37) oceans levels to rise and flood coastal regions.

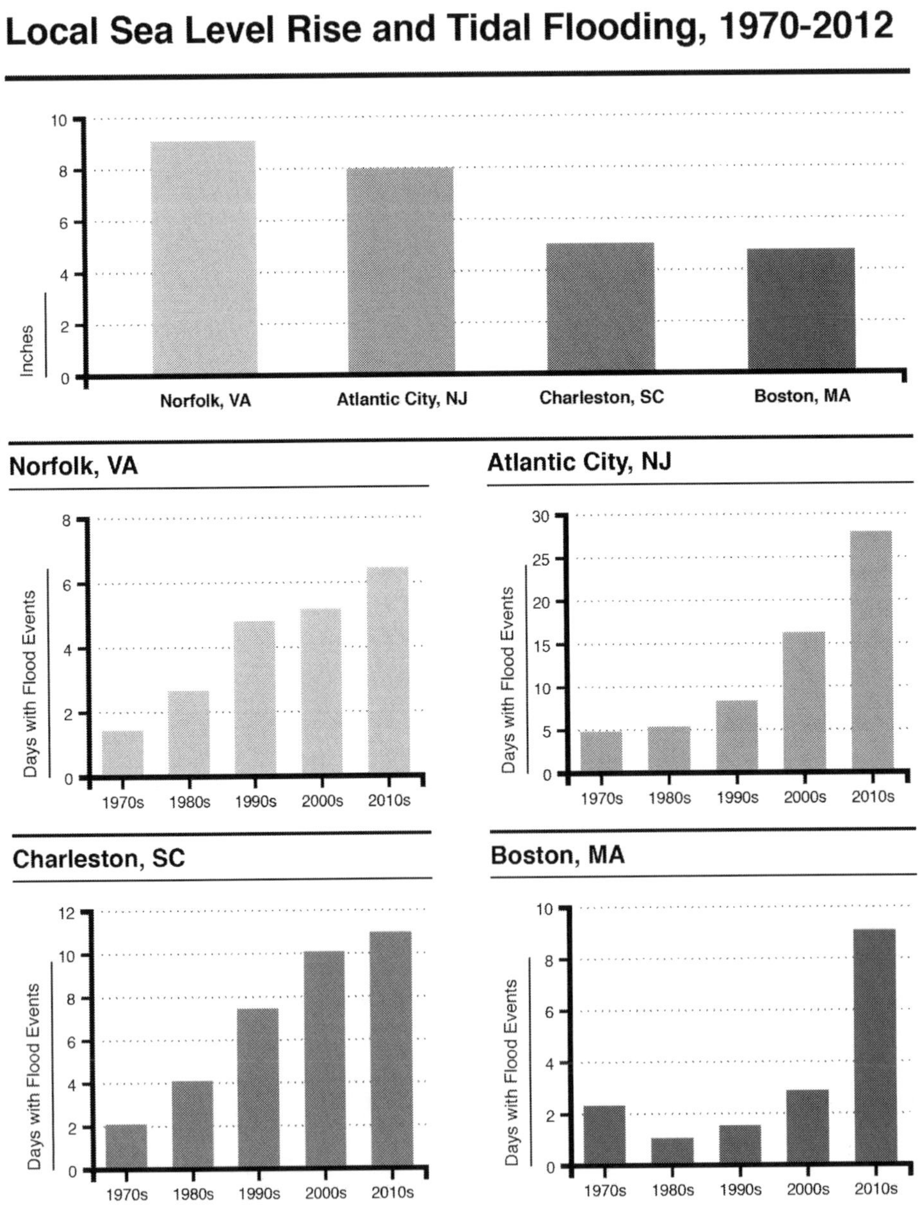

Most commonly, flooding is caused by excessive rain. The ground is not able to absorb all the water produced by a sudden heavy rainfall or rainfall that occurs over a prolonged period of time. Such rainfall may cause the water in rivers and other bodies of water to overflow. The excess water can cause dams to break. Such events can cause flooding of the surrounding riverbanks or coastal regions.

Flash flooding can occur without warning and without rainfall. Flash floods may be caused by a river being blocked by a glacier, avalanche, landslide, logjam, a beaver's obstruction, construction, or dam. Water builds behind such a blockage. Eventually, the mass and force of the built-up water become so extreme that it causes the obstruction to break. Thus, enormous amounts of water rush out towards the surrounding areas.

Areal or urban flooding occurs because the land has become hardened. The hardening of land may result from urbanization or drought. Either way, the hardened land prevents water from seeping into the ground. Instead, the water resides on top of the land.

Finally, flooding may result after severe hurricanes, tsunamis, or tropical cyclones. Local defenses and infrastructures are no matches for the tidal surges and waves caused by these natural phenomena. Such events are bound to result in the flooding of nearby coastal regions or estuaries.

A Floods After-Effects

Flooding can result in severe devastation of nearby areas. Flash floods and tsunamis can result in sweeping waters that travel at destructive speeds. Fast-moving water has the power to demolish all obstacles in its path such as homes, trees, bridges, and buildings. Animals, plants, and humans may all lose their lives during a flood.

Floods can also cause pollution and infection. Sewage may seep from drains or septic tanks and contaminate drinking water or surrounding lands. Similarly, toxins, fuels, debris from annihilated buildings, and other hazardous materials can leave water unusable for consumption. <u>(38) As the water begins to drain, mold may begin to grow.</u> As a result, residents of flooded areas may be left without power, drinkable water, or be exposed to toxins and other diseases.

<u>(39) Although often associated with devastation, not all flooding results</u> in adverse circumstances. For thousands of years, peoples have inhabited floodplains of rivers. <u>(41) Examples include the Mississippi Valley of the United States, the Nile River in Egypt, and the Tigris River of the Middle East</u>. The flooding of such rivers <u>(42) caused</u> nutrient-rich silts to be deposited on the floodplains. Thus, after the floods recede, an extremely fertile soil is left behind. This soil is conducive to the agriculture of bountiful crops and has sustained the diets of humans for millennium.

Proactive Measures Against Flooding

Technologies now allow scientists to predict where and when flooding is likely to occur. Such technologies can also be used (43) <u>to project</u> the severity of an anticipated flood. In this way, local inhabitants can be warned and take preventative measures such as boarding up their homes, gathering necessary provisions, and moving themselves and possessions to higher grounds.

The (44) picturesque views of coastal regions and rivers have long enticed people to build near such locations. Due to the costs associated with the repairs needed after the flooding of such residencies, many governments now require inhabitants of flood-prone areas to purchase flood insurance and build flood-resistant structures. Pictures of all items within a building or home should be taken so that proper reimbursement for losses can be made in the event that a flood does occur.

Staying Safe During a Flood

If a forecasted flood does occur, then people should retreat to higher ground such as a mountain, attic, or roof. Flooded waters may be contaminated, contain hidden debris, or travel at high speeds. Therefore, people should not attempt to walk or drive through a flooded area. To prevent electrocution, electrical outlets and downed power lines need to be avoided.

The Flood Dries Up

Regardless of the type or cause of a flood, floods can result in detrimental alterations to nearby lands and serious injuries to nearby inhabitants. By understanding flood cycles, civilizations can learn to take advantage of flood seasons. By taking the proper precautionary measures, people can stay safe when floods occur. Thus, proper knowledge can lead to safety and prosperity during such an adverse natural phenomenon.

34. What information from the graphs could be used to support the claims found in the third paragraph?
    a. Between 1970-1980, Boston experienced a decrease in the number of days with flood events.
    b. Between 1970-1980, Atlantic City, New Jersey did not experience an increase in the number of days with flood events.
    c. Since 1970, the number of days with floods has decreased in major coastal cities across America.
    d. Since 1970, sea levels have risen along the East Coast.

35. One of the headings is entitled "A Floods After-Effects." How should this heading be rewritten?
    a. A Flood's After-Effect
    b. A Flood's After-Effects
    c. A Floods After-Affect
    d. A Flood's After-Affects

36. Which of the following revisions can be made to the sentence that will still maintain the original meaning while making the sentence more concise?
    a. NO CHANGE
    b. Flooding can either be slow or occur within seconds. It doesn't take long to submerge small regions or extend vast areas of land.
    c. Flooding occurs slowly or rapidly submerging vast areas of land.
    d. Vast areas of land can be flooded slowly or within seconds.

37.
- a. NO CHANGE
- b. Ocean levels
- c. Ocean's levels
- d. Levels of the oceans

38. Which choice best maintains the pattern of the first sentence of the paragraph?
- a. NO CHANGE
- b. As the rain subsides and the water begins to drain, mold may begin to grow.
- c. Mold may begin to grow as the water begins to drain.
- d. The water will begin to drain and mold will begin to grow.

39.
- a. NO CHANGE
- b. Although often associated with devastation not all flooding results
- c. Although often associated with devastation. Not all flooding results
- d. While often associated with devastation, not all flooding results

40. What is the author's intent of the final paragraph?
- a. To explain that all bad occurrences eventually come to an end.
- b. To summarize the key points within the passage.
- c. To explain that, with time, all flooded lands will eventually dry.
- d. To relay a final key point about floods.

41. The author is considering deleting this sentence from the tenth paragraph. Should the sentence be kept or deleted?
- a. Kept, because it provides examples of floodplains that have been successfully inhabited by civilizations.
- b. Kept, because it provides an example of how floods can be beneficial.
- c. Deleted, because it blurs the paragraph's focus on the benefits of floods.
- d. Deleted, because it distracts from the overall meaning of the paragraph.

42.
- a. NO CHANGE
- b. Cause
- c. Causing
- d. Causes

43.
- a. NO CHANGE
- b. Projecting
- c. Project
- d. Projected

44. Which term could best replace the underlined word?
- a. Colorful
- b. Drab
- c. Scenic
- d. Candid

Answer Explanations

1. D: This passage is informative (*D*) because it is nonfiction and factual. The passage's intent is not to state an opinion, discuss an individual's life, or tell a story. Thus, the passage is not argumentative (*A*), biographical (*C*), or narrative (*B*).

2. D: To begin, *of* is not required here. *Apprenticeship* is also more appropriate in this context than *apprentice opportunities, apprentice* describes an individual in an apprenticeship, not an apprenticeship itself. Both of these changes are needed, making (*D*) the correct answer.

3. D: To begin, the selected sentence is a run-on, and displays confusing information. Thus, the sentence does need revision, making (*A*) wrong. The main objective of the selected section of the passage is to communicate that many positions (*positions* is a more suitable term than *offices,* as well) require a PE license, which is gained by scoring well on the FE and PE assessments. This must be the primary focus of the revision. It is necessary to break the sentence into two, to avoid a run-on. Choice *B* fixes the run-on aspect, but the sentence is indirect and awkward in construction. It takes too long to establish the importance of the PE license. Choice *C* is wrong for the same reason and it is a run on. Choice *D* is correct because it breaks the section into coherent sentences and emphasizes the main point the author is trying to communicate: the PE license is required for some higher positions, it's obtained by scoring well on the two standardized assessments, and college and experience can be used to prepare for the assessments in order to gain the certification.

4. C: Any time a writer wants to validate a claim, he or she ought to provide factual information that proves or supports that claim: "beginning his or her preparation for the profession in high school" supports the claim that aircraft engineers undergo years of education. For this reason, Choice *C* is the correct response. However, completing such courses in high school does not guarantee that aircraft engineers will earn generous salaries (*A*), become employed in executive positions (*B*), or stay employed (*D*).

5. B: Choice *B* is correct because "skill" is defined as having certain aptitude for a given task. (*C*) is incorrect because "work" does not directly denote "critical thinking, business skills, problem solving, and creativity." (*A*) is incorrect because the word "care" doesn't fit into the context of the passage, and (*D*), "composition," is incorrect because nothing in this statement points to the way in which something is structured.

6. C: *Allows* is inappropriate because it does not stress what those in the position of aircraft engineers actually need to be able to do. *Requires* is the only alternative that fits because it actually describes necessary skills of the job.

7. B: The third paragraph discusses reports made by the United States Bureau of Labor Statistics (BLS) in regards to the median, upper 10 percent, and lower 10 percent annual salaries of aircraft engineers in 2015. Therefore, this paragraph is used to support the claim that aircraft engineers are compensated with generous salaries (*B*). The paragraph has nothing to do with an aircraft engineer's skill set (*A*), education (*C*), or incentive program (*D*).

8. A: The correct response is (*A*) because this statement's intent is to give examples as to how aircraft engineers apply mathematical equations and scientific processes towards aeronautical and aerospace issues and/or inventions. The answer is not "therefore" (*B*) or "furthermore" (*D*) because no causality is being made between ideas. Two items are neither being compared nor contrasted, so “however” (*C*) is also not the correct answer.

9. A: No change is required. The comma is properly placed after the introductory phrase “In May of 2015.” Choice *B* is missing the word “in.” Choice *C* does not separate the introductory phrase from the rest of the sentence. Choice *D* places an extra, and unnecessary, comma prior to 2015.

10. A: The word “conversely” best demonstrates the opposite sentiments in this passage. Choice *B* is incorrect because it denotes agreement with the previous statement. Choice *C* is incorrect because the sentiment is not restated but opposed. Choice *D* is incorrect because the previous statement is not a cause for the sentence in question.

11. A: Choice *A* is the correct answer because the projections are taking place in the present, even though they are making reference to a future date.

12. B: The passage contains clearly labeled subheadings. These subheadings inform the reader what will be addressed in upcoming paragraphs. Choice *A* is incorrect because the anti-terrorism laws of other countries were never addressed in the passage. The text is written in an informative manner; overly descriptive language is not utilized. Therefore, Choice *C* is incorrect. Choice *D* is incorrect because as mentioned, the structure of the text does help in the manner described in Choice *B*.

13. A: No change is needed. Choices *B* and *C* utilize incorrect comma placements. Choice *D* utilizes an incorrect verb tense (responding).

14. D: The third paragraph states “The majority of Muslims practice Islam peacefully”. Therefore, the author explicitly states that most Muslims are peaceful peoples (*D*). Choices *B*, *C*, and *A* are not included in the passage and are incorrect.

15. B: The term “violate” implies a lack of respect or compliance. “Defile” means to degrade or show no respect. Therefore, (*B*) is the correct answer. Choice *A* is incorrect because “respect” is the opposite of violate. To “deny” is to refuse, so (*C*) is not the answer because the weight of the word “deny” is not as heavy as the word “violate.” To “obey” is to follow orders, so (*D*) is not the answer.

16. B: An allusion is a direct or indirect literary reference or figure of speech towards a person, place, or event. By referencing the diversion of the airplanes to alternate locations, the author uses an allusion (Choice *B*) to highlight the impact of United Flight 93. Although a graph depicting the decline in the number of aircraft passengers is provided, an image is not. Therefore, Choice *A* is not the answer. The passage does not tell the story from a single passenger’s point of view. Thus, Choice *C* and Choice *D* are not the answers.

17. C: All of the choices except (*C*) go with the flow of the original underlined portion of the sentence and communicate the same idea. Choice *C*, however, does not take into account the rest of the sentence and therefore, becomes awkward and incorrect.

18. B: Although “diverging” means to separate from the main route and go in a different direction, it is used awkwardly and unconventionally in this sentence. Therefore, Choice *A* is not the answer. Choice *B* is the correct answer because it implies that the passengers distracted the terrorists, which caused a change in the plane’s direction. “Converging” (*C*) is incorrect because it implies that the plane met another in a central location. Although the passengers may have distracted the terrorists, they did not distract the plane. Therefore, Choice *D* is incorrect.

19. D: The graph shows the number of people (in millions) boarding United States' flights between 1996-2005. The graph includes a vertical red line that indicates the dip in the number people that boarded U.S. flights on September 11, 2001. Therefore, the graph illustrates the effects of suspending air travel immediately after the attacks (*D*). The graph does not show where the flights were redirected (*B*), the number of passengers that other countries received as a result of the redirected air travel (*C*), or the resulting flight schedule implications (Choice *A*).

20. B: The last paragraph explains that museums and monuments have been erected to honor those who died as a result of the attacks and those who risked their lives to save the injured. Thus, the paragraph serves to explain the lasting impact on America and honor those impacted by the event (*B*). The design of the museums and monuments are not described, so Choice *A* is incorrect. Choice *C* is incorrect because America's War on Terror was not discussed in the last paragraph. Choice *D* is incorrect, because although the previous location of the towers was converted into a park, this was not mentioned in the passage.

21. C: *Intended* means planned or meant to. *Intended* is a far better choice than *desired*, because it would communicate goals and strategy more than simply saying that Bush desired to do something. *Desired* communicates wishing or direct motive. Choices B and D have irrelevant meanings and wouldn't serve the sentence at all.

22. A: While (*B*) isn't necessarily wrong, it lacks the direct nature that the original sentence has. Also, by breaking up the sentences like this, the reader becomes confused because the connection between the Taliban's defeat and ongoing war is now separated by a second sentence that is not necessary. Choice *C* corrects this problem but the fluidity of the sentence is marred because of the awkward construction of the first sentence. Choice *D* begins well, but lacks the use of *was* before overthrown, which discombobulates the sentence. While *yet* provides an adequate transition for the next sentence, the term *however* is more appropriate. Thus, the original structure of the two sentences is correct, making Choice *A*, NO CHANGE, the correct answer.

23. A: The comma after *result* is necessary for the sentence structure, making it an imperative component. The original sentence is correct, making Choice *A* correct. For the reason just listed, Choice *B* is incorrect because it lacks the crucial comma that introduces a new idea. Choice *C* is incorrect because a colon is unnecessary, and Choice *D* is wrong because the addition of "of" is both unnecessary and incorrect when applied to the rest of the sentence.

24. C: To be "gifted" is to be talented. "Academically" refers to education. Therefore, Fred Hampton was intellectually talented, or intelligent (*C*). Choice *B* is incorrect because it refers to a level of energy or activity. Choice *A* is incorrect because "vacuous" means the opposite of being gifted academically. Choice *D* is incorrect because it refers to one's physical build and/or abilities.

25. C: The goal for this question is to select a sentence that not only affirms, or backs up, the selected statement, but could also appear after it and flows with the rest of the piece. Choice *A* is irrelevant to the sentence; just because new members earned scholarships this doesn't necessarily mean that this was testament of Hampton's leadership or that this actually benefitted the NAACP. Choice *B* is very compelling. If Hampton got an award for the increase in numbers, this could bolster the idea that he was the direct cause of the rise in numbers and that he was of great value to the organization. However, it does not say directly that he was the cause of the increase and that this was extremely beneficial to the NAACP. Let's keep looking. Choice *C* is a much better choice than Choice *B*. Choice *C* has the new members directly accrediting Hampton for his leadership; the fact that such new members went on to hold high positions is also testament to Hampton's leadership. Thus, Choice *C* is correct. Choice *D* does nothing for the underlined section.

26. B: Choice *B* moves the word "eventually" to the beginning of the sentences. By using the term as an introductory word, continuity from one sentence to another is created. Meanwhile, the syntax is not lost. Choice *A* is incorrect because the sentence requires a proper transition. Choice *C* is incorrect because the sentence does not contain surprising or contrasting information, as is indicated by the introductory word "nevertheless." Choice *D* is incorrect -because the term "then" implies that Hampton's relocation to the BPP's headquarters in Chicago occurred shortly or immediately after leading the NAACP.

27. D: An individual with a charismatic personality is charming and appealing to others. Therefore, Choice *D* is the correct answer. Choice A is incorrect because someone with an egotistical personality is conceited or self-serving. Choice *B* is incorrect because "obnoxious" is the opposite of charismatic. Choice *C* is incorrect because someone with a chauvinistic personality is aggressive or prejudiced towards one's purpose, desire, or sex.

28. A: No change is needed: Choice *A*. The list of events accomplished by Hampton is short enough that each item in the list can be separated by a comma. Choice *B* is incorrect. Although a colon can be used to introduce a list of items, it is not a conventional choice for separating items within a series. Semicolons are used to separate at least three items in a series that have an internal comma. Semicolons can also be used to separate clauses in a sentence that contain internal commas intended for clarification purposes. Neither of the two latter uses of semicolons is required in the example sentence. Therefore, Choice *C* is incorrect. Choice *D* is incorrect because a dash is not a conventional choice for punctuating items in a series.

29. D: Claims can be supported with evidence or supporting details found within the text. Choice *D* is correct because Choices *A*, *B*, and *C* are all either directly stated or alluded to within the passage.

30. A: The term *neutralize* means to counteract, or render ineffective, which is exactly what the FBI is wanting to do. Accommodate means to be helpful or lend aid, which is the opposite of *neutralize*. Therefore (*B*) is wrong. *Assuage* means to ease, while *praise* means to express warm feeling, so they are in no way close to the needed context. Therefore, *neutralize* is the best option, making Choice *A*, NO CHANGE, the correct answer.

31. B: The order of the original sentence suggests that the floor plans that were provided to the FBI by O'Neal enabled the FBI to identify the exact location of Hampton's bed. This syntax is maintained in Choice *B*. Therefore, Choice *B* is correct, which makes Choice *A* incorrect. Choice *C* is incorrect because the sentence's word order conveys the meaning that O'Neal provided the FBI with Hampton's bed as well as the floor plans. Choice *D* is incorrect because it implies that it was the location of the bed that provided the FBI with the headquarters' floor plans.

32. B: "Commemorates" means to honor, celebrate, or memorialize a person or event. Therefore, Choice *B* is correct. Choice *A* is incorrect because "disregards" is the opposite of "commemorates." Choice *C* is incorrect because to communicate means to converse or to speak. Choice *D* is incorrect because to "deny" means to reject, negate, refuse, or rebuff.

33. D: From the context of the passage, it is clear that the author does not think well of the FBI and their investigation of Hampton and the Black Panthers. Choices *B* and *C* can be easily eliminated. "Well intended" is positive, which is not a characteristic that he would probably attribute to the FBI in the passage. Nor would he think they were "confused" but deliberate in their methods. Choice *A,* "corrupt", is very compelling; he'd likely agree with this, but Choice *D,* "prejudiced" is better. The FBI may not have been corrupt but there certainly seemed to have particular dislike/distrust for the Black Panthers. Thus, Choice *D*, "prejudiced", is correct.

34. D: All of the cities included in the graphs are along the East Coast of the United States. All of the bars on the graphs show an increase in sea level or the number of days with flood events since 1970. Therefore, the author chose to include the graphs to support the claim that sea levels have risen along the East Coast since 1970, choice D. Choice *A* and Choice *B* are incorrect because the bars above 1970 on Boston's graph and Atlantic City's graph are shorter than the graphs' bars above 1980. Therefore, between 1970-1980, both cities experienced an increase in the number of days with flood events. Choice *C* is incorrect because the bars increase in height on all of the cities' graphs, showing an increase in the number of days with floods along the entire East coast.

35. B: Although "affect" and "effect" sound the same, they have different meanings. "Affect" is used as a verb. It is defined as the influence of a person, place, or event on another. "Effect" is used as a noun. It is defined as the result of an event. Therefore, the latter ought to be used in the heading. For this reason, Choices *C* and *D* are incorrect. Because the effect is a result of the flood, a possessive apostrophe is needed for the singular noun "flood." For this reason, Choice *A* is incorrect and Choice *B* is correct.

36. D: Again, the objective for questions like this is to determine if a revision is possible within the choices and if it can adhere to the specific criteria of the question; in this case, we want the sentence to maintain the original meaning while being more concise, or shorter. Choice *B* can be eliminated. The meaning of the original sentence is split into two distinct sentences. The second of the two sentences is also incorrectly constructed. Choice *C* is very intriguing but there is a jumble of verbs present in: "Flooding occurs slowly or rapidly submerging" that it makes the sentence awkward and difficult to understand without the use of a comma after *rapidly*, making it a poor construction. Choice *C* is wrong. Choice *D* is certainly more concise and it is correctly phrased; it communicates the meaning message that flooding can overtake great lengths of land either slowly or very fast. The use of "Vast areas of land" infers that smaller regions or small areas can flood just as well. Thus, Choice *D* is a good revision that maintains the meaning of the original sentence while being concise and more direct. This rules out Choice *A* in the process.

37. B: In this sentence, the word *ocean* does not require an *s* after it to make it plural because "ocean levels" is plural. Therefore (*A*) and (*C*) are incorrect. Because the passage is referring to multiple – if not all ocean levels – *ocean* does not require an apostrophe (*'s*) because that would indicate that only one ocean is the focus, which is not the case. Choice *D* does not fit well into the sentence and, once again, we see that *ocean* has an *s* after it. This leaves Choice *B,* which correctly completes the sentence and maintains the intended meaning.

38. C: Choice *C* is the best answer because it most closely maintains the sentence pattern of the first sentence of the paragraph, which begins with a noun and passive verb phrase. Choice *A* and *C* are incorrect. Choice *B* is incorrect because it does not maintain the sentence pattern of the first sentence of the paragraph. Instead, Choice *B* shifts the placement of the modifying prepositional phrase to the beginning of the sentence. Choice *D* is incorrect because it does not maintain the sentence pattern established by the first sentence of the paragraph. Instead, Choice *D* is an attempt to combine two independent clauses.

39. A: Choice *C* can be eliminated because creating a new sentence with *not* is grammatically incorrect and it throws off the rest of the sentence. Choice *B* is wrong because a comma is definitely needed after *devastation* in the sentence. Choice *D* is also incorrect because "while" is a poor substitute for "although". *Although* in this context is meant to show contradiction with the idea that floods are associated with devastation. Therefore, none of these choices would be suitable revisions because the original was correct: NO CHANGE, Choice *A,* is the correct answer.

40. B: Choice *B* is the correct answer because the final paragraph summarizes key points from each subsection of the text. Therefore, the final paragraph serves as the conclusion. A concluding paragraph is often found at the end of a text. It serves to remind the reader of the main points of a text. Choice *A* is incorrect because the last paragraph does not just mention adverse effects of floods. For example, the paragraph states "By understanding flood cycles, civilizations can learn to take advantage of flood seasons." Choice *C* is incorrect; although the subheading mentions the drying of floods, the phenomena is not mentioned in the paragraph. Finally, Choice *D* is incorrect because no new information is presented in the last paragraph of the passage.

41. A: Idea and claims are best expressed and supported within a text through examples, evidence, and descriptions. Choice *A* is correct because it provides examples of rivers that support the tenth paragraph's claim that "not all flooding results in adverse circumstances." Choice *B* is incorrect because the sentence does not explain how floods are beneficial. Therefore, Choices *C* and *D* are incorrect.

42. D: In the sentence, *caused* is an incorrect tense, making (*A*) wrong. Choice *B* is incorrect because this used as a noun, we need *cause* in verb form. Choices *C* and *D* are very compelling. *Causing* (*C*) is a verb and it is in the present continuous tense, which appears to agree with the verb flooding, but it is incorrectly used. This leaves (*D*), *causes*, which does fit because it is in the indefinite present tense. Fitting each choice into the sentence and reading it in your mind will also reveal that (*D*), *causes*, correctly completes the sentence. Apply this method to all the questions when possible.

43. A: To *project* means to anticipate or forecast. This goes very well with the sentence because it describes how new technology is trying to estimate flood activity in order to prevent damage and save lives. "Project" in this case needs to be assisted by "to" in order to function in the sentence. Therefore, Choice *A* is correct. Choices *B* and *D* are the incorrect tenses. Choice *C* is also wrong because it lacks *to*.

44. C: *Picturesque* is an adjective used for an attractive, scenic, or otherwise striking image. Thus, Choice *C* is correct. Choice *A* is incorrect because although "colorful" can be included in a picturesque view, it does not encompass the full meaning of the word. Choice *B* is incorrect because "drab" is the opposite of "picturesque." Choice *D* is incorrect because "candid" is defined as being frank, open, truthful, or honest.

Essay

Introduction to the SAT Essay

The essay on the SAT is now optional, although some schools do require that you write the essay for application. Test takers will have fifty minutes to write their essay. In the format of the SAT essay, you will be given an essay to read and analyze. Keep in mind that you will not be asked to agree or disagree on the topic of the essay or even write about the topic of the essay. You will be asked to write about how the author built that essay and which rhetorical devices they used throughout the essay. Viewers of your essay will be looking for ways in which you explain how the author creates their argument in order to persuade an audience, and you will be expected to support your ideas with evidence from the passage.

Analyzing the Essay

In the prompt of the SAT essay, you will be asked to consider the following three characteristics of an essay: the author's evidence, reasoning, and stylistic elements. The sections below give a description of what to look for in each of these.

Evidence

It's important to evaluate the author's supporting details to be sure that the details are credible, provide evidence of the author's point, and directly support the main idea. Though shocking statistics grab readers' attention, their use could be ineffective information in the piece. Details like this are crucial to understanding the passage and evaluating how well the author presents their argument and evidence.

Fact and Opinion

It is important to distinguish between *fact and opinion* when reading a piece of writing. When an author presents *facts*, such as statistics or data, readers must make sure they are accurate. When authors use *opinion*, they are sharing their own thoughts and feelings about a subject.

Textual evidence within the details helps readers draw a conclusion about a passage. *Textual evidence* refers to information—facts and examples that support the main point. Textual evidence will likely come from outside sources and can be in the form of quoted or paraphrased material. In order to draw a conclusion from evidence, it's important to examine the credibility and validity of that evidence as well as how (and if) it relates to the main idea.

Credibility

Critical readers examine the facts used to support an author's argument. They check the facts against other sources to be sure those facts are correct. They also check the validity of the sources used to be sure those sources are credible, academic, and/or peer-reviewed. Consider that when an author uses another person's opinion to support their argument, even if it is an expert's opinion, it is still only an opinion and should not be taken as fact. A strong argument uses valid, measurable facts to support ideas. Even then, the reader may disagree with the argument as it may be rooted in their personal beliefs.

An authoritative argument may use the facts to sway the reader. In the example of global warming, many experts differ in their opinions of what alternative fuels can be used to aid in offsetting it. Because of this, a writer may choose to only use the information and expert opinion that supports their viewpoint.

Reasoning

Reasoning has to do with the way the author develops ideas and connects claims and evidence. For this, it's importance to pay attention to the overall structure of the passage. If the passage is sound, the author will use effective transition words that guide the logical progression of the points. A term like *however* alerts the reader that the author is about to present information in contrast to the information presented before. Likewise, if the author were presenting cause/effect, some transition words used might be *because, since, for,* or *due to*. If these transition words are absent, then logical progression of the text is lacking and the author is using an ineffective structure to present his or her argument.

Counter-Arguments

If an author presents a differing opinion or a *counter-argument* in order to refute it, the reader should consider how and why this information is being presented. It is meant to strengthen the original argument and shouldn't be confused with the author's intended conclusion, but it should also be considered in the reader's final evaluation. On the contrary, sometimes authors will concede to an opposing argument by recognizing the validity the other side has to offer. A concession will allow readers to see both sides of the argument in an unbiased light, thereby increasing the credibility of the author.

Authors can also reflect *bias* if they ignore an opposing viewpoint or present their side in an unbalanced way. A strong argument considers the opposition and finds a way to refute it. Critical readers should look for an unfair or one-sided presentation of the argument and be skeptical, as a bias may be present. Even if this bias is unintentional, if it exists in the writing, the reader should be wary of the validity of the argument.

Stylistic Elements

Stylistic elements are elements an author uses in order to convey meaning to the text in unique ways. Some of these different ways are appealing to the audience's emotion, the author's word choice, and figurative language.

Appeal to Emotion

The audience is what determines the *rhetorical appeal* the author will use—ethos, pathos, or logos. *Ethos* is a rhetorical appeal to an audience's ethics and/or morals. Ethos is most often used in argumentative and informative writing modes. *Pathos* is an appeal to the audience's emotions and sympathies, and it is found in argumentative, descriptive, and narrative writing modes. *Logos* is an appeal to the audience's logic and reason and is used primarily in informative texts as well as in supporting details for argumentative pieces.

Word Choice

An author's choice of words—also referred to as *diction*—helps to convey his or her meaning in a particular way. Through diction, an author can convey a particular tone—e.g., a humorous tone, a serious tone—in order to support the thesis in a meaningful way to the reader.

Connotation refers to the implied meaning of a word or phrase. Connotations are the ideas or feelings that words or phrase invoke other than their literal meaning. An example of the use of connotation is in people's use of the word *cheap*. While the literal meaning is something of low cost, people use the word to suggest something is poor in value or to negatively describe a person as reluctant to spend money.

When something or someone is described this way, the reader is more inclined to have a particular image or feeling about it or him/her. Thus, connotation can be a very effective language tool in creating emotion and swaying opinion. However, connotations are sometimes hard to pin down because varying emotions can be associated with a word. Generally, though, connotative meanings tend to be fairly consistent within a specific cultural group.

Test takers and critical readers alike should be very aware of *technical language* used within informational text. *Technical language* refers to terminology that is specific to a particular industry and is best understood by those specializing in that industry. This language is fairly easy to differentiate, since it will most likely be unfamiliar to readers. It's critical to be able to define technical language either by the author's written definition, through the use of an included glossary—if offered—or through context clues that help readers clarify word meaning.

Figurative Language
Literary texts also employ rhetorical devices. Figurative language like simile and metaphor is a type of rhetorical device commonly found in literature. In addition to rhetorical devices that play on the *meanings* of words, there are also rhetorical devices that use the *sounds* of words. These devices are most often found in poetry but may also be found in other types of literature and in non-fiction writing like speech texts.

Alliteration and *assonance* are both varieties of sound repetition. Other types of sound repetition include: anaphora, repetition that occurs at the beginning of the sentences; epiphora, repetition occurring at the end of phrases; antimetabole, repetition of words in reverse order; and antiphrasis, a form of denial of an assertion in a text.

Alliteration refers to the repetition of the first sound of each word. Recall Robert Burns' opening line:

> My love is like a red, red rose

This line includes two instances of alliteration: "love" and "like" (repeated *L* sound), as well as "red" and "rose" (repeated *R* sound). Next, assonance refers to the repetition of vowel sounds, and can occur anywhere within a word (not just the opening sound). Here is the opening of a poem by John Keats:

> When I have fears that I may cease to be
> Before my pen has glean'd my teeming brain

Assonance can be found in the words "fears," "cease," "be," "glean'd," and "teeming," all of which stress the long *E* sound. Both alliteration and assonance create a harmony that unifies the writer's language.

Another sound device is *onomatopoeia*, or words whose spelling mimics the sound they describe. Words like "crash," "bang," and "sizzle" are all examples of onomatopoeia. Use of onomatopoetic language adds auditory imagery to the text.

Readers are probably most familiar with the technique of *pun*. A pun is a play on words, taking advantage of two words that have the same or similar pronunciation. Puns can be found throughout Shakespeare's plays, for instance:

> Now is the winter of our discontent
> Made glorious summer by this son of York

These lines from *Richard III* contain a play on words. Richard III refers to his brother, the newly crowned King Edward IV, as the "son of York," referencing their family heritage from the house of York. However, while drawing a comparison between the political climate and the weather (times of political trouble were the "winter," but now the new king brings "glorious summer"), Richard's use of the word "son" also implies another word with the same pronunciation, "sun"—so Edward IV is also like the sun, bringing light, warmth, and hope to England. Puns are a clever way for writers to suggest two meanings at once.

Writing the Essay

Brainstorming

One of the most important steps in writing an essay is prewriting. Before drafting an essay, it's helpful to think about the topic for a moment or two, in order to gain a more solid understanding of what the task is. Then, spending about five minutes jotting down the immediate ideas that could work for the essay is recommended. This serves as a way to get some words on the page and offer a reference for ideas when drafting. Scratch paper is provided for writers to use any prewriting techniques such as webbing, free writing, or listing. The goal is to get ideas out of the mind and onto the page.

Moving from Brainstorming to Planning

Once the ideas are on the page, it's time to turn them into a solid plan for the essay. The best ideas from the brainstorming results can then be developed into a more formal outline. An outline typically has one main point (the thesis) and at least three sub-points that support the main point.

Here's an example:

Main Idea

- Point #1
- Point #2
- Point #3

Of course, there will be details under each point, but this approach is the best for dealing with timed writing.

Time Management

It is important to manage your time effectively. It is recommended that you allocate time at the beginning of your writing to review the prompt and instructions multiple times and then outline your basic thoughts, either on paper or in your head. This initial thinking process will give you a clear plan of action before you put pen to paper and will result in a more concise and effective argument.

Similarly, it is recommended that you leave a few minutes at the end of your writing to review your piece and ensure it is coherent, includes examples that support each of your key argument points, and specifically addresses the instructions that were provided. Clarity of thought and staying focused on the topic that you were asked to write about are more important than citing every example you can think of that supports your argument in excruciating detail.

Parts of the Essay

The *introduction* has to do a few important things:

- Establish the *topic* of the essay in original wording (i.e., not just repeating the prompt)
- Clarify the significance/importance of the topic or purpose for writing (not too many details, a brief overview)
- Offer a *thesis statement* that identifies the writer's own viewpoint on the topic (typically one or two brief sentences as a clear, concise explanation of the main point on the topic)

Body paragraphs reflect the ideas developed in the outline. Three or four points is probably sufficient for a short essay, and they should include the following:

- A *topic sentence* that identifies the sub-point (e.g., a reason why, a way how, a cause or effect)
- A detailed *explanation* of the point, explaining why the writer thinks this point is valid
- Illustrative *examples*, such as personal examples or real-world examples, that support and validate the point (i.e., "prove" the point)
- A *concluding sentence* that connects the examples, reasoning, and analysis to the point being made

The *conclusion*, or final paragraph, should be brief and should reiterate the focus, clarifying why the discussion is significant or important. It is important to avoid adding specific details or new ideas to this paragraph. The purpose of the conclusion is to sum up what has been said to bring the discussion to a close.

Don't Panic!

Writing an essay can be overwhelming, and performance panic is a natural response. The outline serves as a basis for the writing and help writers stay focused. Getting stuck can also happen, and it's helpful to remember that brainstorming can be done at any time during the writing process. Following the steps of the writing process is the best defense against writer's block.

Timed essays can be particularly stressful, but assessors are trained to recognize the necessary planning and thinking for these timed efforts. Using the plan above, and sticking to it, helps with time management. Timing each part of the process helps writers stay on track. Sometimes writers try to cover too much in their essays. If time seems to be running out, writers should take the opportunity to determine whether all of the ideas in the outline are necessary. Three body paragraphs are sufficient, and more than that is probably too much to cover in a short essay.

More isn't always *better* in writing. A strong essay will be clear and concise. It will avoid unnecessary or repetitive details. It is better to have a concise, five-paragraph essay that makes a clear point, than a ten-paragraph essay that doesn't. The goal is to write one to two pages of quality writing. Paragraphs should also reflect balance; if the introduction goes to the bottom of the first page, the writing may be going off-track or be repetitive. It's best to fall into the one-to-two-page range, but a complete, well-developed essay is the ultimate goal.

The Final Steps

Leaving a few minutes at the end to revise and proofread offers an opportunity for writers to polish things up. Putting oneself in the reader's shoes and focusing on what the essay actually says helps writers identify problems—it's a movement from the mindset of the writer to the mindset of the editor. The goal is to have a clean, clear copy of the essay. The following areas should be considered when proofreading:

- Sentence fragments
- Awkward sentence structure
- Run-on sentences
- Incorrect word choice
- Grammatical agreement errors
- Spelling errors
- Punctuation errors
- Capitalization errors

The Short Overview

The essay may seem challenging, but following these steps can help writers focus:

- Take one-two minutes to think about the topic.
- Generate some ideas through brainstorming (three-four minutes).
- Organize ideas into a brief outline, selecting just three-four main points to cover in the essay
- Develop essay in parts:
- Introduction paragraph, with intro to topic and main points
- Viewpoint on the subject at the end of the introduction
- Body paragraphs, based on outline
- Each paragraph: makes a main point, explains the viewpoint, uses examples to support the point
- Brief conclusion highlighting the main points and closing
- Read over the essay (last five minutes).
- Look for any obvious errors, making sure that the writing makes sense.

Essay Prompt #1

As you read the essay below, consider how the author uses these following things:

- Evidence to support claims, like facts or examples
- Reasoning to develop ideas and connect claims to evidence
- Stylistic elements, such as word choice or appeals to emotion, to express ideas

Dana Gioia argues in his article that poetry is dying, now little more than a limited art form confined to academic and college settings. Of course poetry remains healthy in the academic setting, but the idea of poetry being limited to this academic subculture is a stretch. New technology and social networking alone have contributed to poets and other writers' work being shared across the world. YouTube has emerged to be a major asset to poets, allowing live performances to be streamed to billions of users. Even now, poetry continues to grow and voice topics that are relevant to the culture of our time. Poetry is not in the spotlight as it may have been in earlier times, but it's still a relevant art form that continues to expand in scope and appeal.

Furthermore, Gioia's argument does not account for live performances of poetry. Not everyone has taken a poetry class or enrolled in university—but most everyone is online. The Internet is a perfect launching point to get all creative work out there. An example of this was the performance of Buddy Wakefield's *Hurling Crowbirds at Mockingbars*. Wakefield is a well-known poet who has published several collections of contemporary poetry. One of my favorite works by Wakefield is *Crowbirds*, specifically his performance at New York University in 2009. Although his reading was a campus event, views of his performance online number in the thousands. His poetry attracted people outside of the university setting.

Naturally, the poem's popularity can be attributed both to Wakefield's performance and the quality of his writing. *Crowbirds* touches on themes of core human concepts such as faith, personal loss, and growth. These are not ideas that only poets or students of literature understand, but all human beings: "You acted like I was hurling crowbirds at mockingbars / and abandoned me for not making sense. / Evidently, I don't experience things as rationally as you do" (Wakefield 15-17). Wakefield weaves together a complex description of the perplexed and hurt emotions of the speaker undergoing a separation from a romantic interest. The line "You acted like I was hurling crowbirds at mockingbars" conjures up an image of someone confused, seemingly out of their mind . . . or in the case of the speaker, passionately trying to grasp at a relationship that is fading. The speaker is looking back and finding the words that described how he wasn't making sense. This poem is particularly human and gripping in its message, but the entire effect of the poem is enhanced through the physical performance.

At its core, poetry is about addressing issues/ideas in the world. Part of this is also addressing the perspectives that are exiguously considered. Although the platform may look different, poetry continues to have a steady audience due to the emotional connection the poet shares with the audience.

Write an essay in which you explain how the author builds an argument to persuade the audience that poetry is not dying. In your essay, analyze how the author uses one or more of the features listed in the bullet points above (or features of your own choice) to strengthen the logic and persuasiveness of their argument. Focus on the most relevant features of the passage.

Reading Test

This article discusses the famous poet and playwright William Shakespeare. Read it and answer questions 1–8.

People who argue that William Shakespeare isn't responsible for the plays attributed to his name are known as anti-Stratfordians (from the name of Shakespeare's birthplace, Stratford-upon-Avon). The most common anti-Stratfordian claim is that William Shakespeare simply was not educated enough or from a high enough social class to have written plays overflowing with references to such a wide range of subjects like history, the classics, religion, and international culture. William Shakespeare was the son of a glove-maker, he only had a basic grade school education, and he never set foot outside of England—so how could he have produced plays of such sophistication and imagination? How could he have written in such detail about historical figures and events, or about different cultures and locations around Europe? According to anti-Stratfordians, the depth of knowledge contained in Shakespeare's plays suggests a well-traveled writer from a wealthy background with a university education, not a countryside writer like Shakespeare. But in fact, there isn't much substance to such speculation, and most anti-Stratfordian arguments can be refuted with a little background about Shakespeare's time and upbringing.

First of all, those who doubt Shakespeare's authorship often point to his common birth and brief education as stumbling blocks to his writerly genius. Although it's true that Shakespeare did not come from a noble class, his father was a very *successful* glove-maker and his mother was from a very wealthy land-owning family—so while Shakespeare may have had a country upbringing, he was certainly from a well-off family and would have been educated accordingly. Also, even though he did not attend university, grade school education in Shakespeare's time was actually quite rigorous and exposed students to classic drama through writers like Seneca and Ovid. It's not unreasonable to believe that Shakespeare received a very solid foundation in poetry and literature from his early schooling.

Next, anti-Stratfordians tend to question how Shakespeare could write so extensively about countries and cultures he had never visited before (for example, several of his most famous works like *Romeo and Juliet* and *The Merchant of Venice* were set in Italy, on the opposite side of Europe). But again, this criticism doesn't hold up under scrutiny. For one thing, Shakespeare was living in London, a bustling metropolis of international trade, the most populous city in England, and a political and cultural hub of Europe. In the daily crowds of people, Shakespeare would certainly have been able to meet travelers from other countries and hear firsthand accounts of life in their home country. And, in addition to the influx of information from world travelers, this was also the age of the printing press, a jump in technology that made it possible to print and circulate books much more easily than in the past. This also allowed for a freer flow of information across different countries, allowing people to read about life and ideas throughout Europe. One needn't travel the continent in order to learn and write about its culture.

1. The main purpose of this article is to:

   a. Explain two sides of an argument and allow readers to choose which side they agree with
   b. Encourage readers to be skeptical about the authorship of famous poems and plays
   c. Give historical background about an important literary figure
   d. Criticize a theory by presenting counterevidence

2. Which sentence contains the author's thesis?

   a. "People who argue that William Shakespeare isn't responsible for the plays attributed to his name are known as anti-Stratfordians."
   b. "But in fact, there isn't much substance to such speculation, and most anti-Stratfordian arguments can be refuted with a little background about Shakespeare's time and upbringing."
   c. "It's not unreasonable to believe that Shakespeare received a very solid foundation in poetry and literature from his early schooling."
   d. "Next, anti-Stratfordians tend to question how Shakespeare could write so extensively about countries and cultures he had never visited before."

3. In the first paragraph, "How could he have written in such detail about historical figures and events, or about different cultures and locations around Europe?" is an example of which of the following?

   a. Hyperbole
   b. Onomatopoeia
   c. Rhetorical question
   d. Appeal to authority

4. How does the author respond to the claim that Shakespeare was not well-educated because he didn't attend university?

   a. By insisting upon Shakespeare's natural genius
   b. By explaining grade school curriculum in Shakespeare's time
   c. By comparing Shakespeare with other uneducated writers of his time
   d. By pointing out that Shakespeare's wealthy parents probably paid for private tutors

5. The word "bustling" in the third paragraph most nearly means:

   a. Busy
   b. Foreign
   c. Expensive
   d. Undeveloped

6. What can be inferred from the article?

   a. Shakespeare's peers were jealous of his success and wanted to attack his reputation.
   b. Until recently, classical drama was only taught in universities.
   c. International travel was extremely rare in Shakespeare's time.
   d. In Shakespeare's time, glove-makers weren't part of the upper class.

7. Why does the author mention *Romeo and Juliet*?

   a. It's Shakespeare's most famous play.
   b. It was inspired by Shakespeare's trip to Italy.
   c. It's an example of a play set outside of England.
   d. It was unpopular when Shakespeare first wrote it.

8. Which statement would the author probably agree with?
   a. It's possible to learn things from reading rather than firsthand experience.
   b. If you want to be truly cultured, you need to travel the world.
   c. People never become successful without a university education.
   d. All of the world's great art comes from Italy.

A traveler prepares for a journey in this excerpt from a novel. Read it and answer questions 9–14.

> When I got on the coach the driver had not taken his seat, and I saw him talking with the landlady. They were evidently talking of me, for every now and then they looked at me, and some of the people who were sitting on the bench outside the door came and listened, and then looked at me, most of them pityingly. I could hear a lot of words often repeated, queer words, for there were many nationalities in the crowd; so I quietly got my polyglot dictionary from my bag and looked them out. I must say they weren't cheering to me, for amongst them were "Ordog"—Satan, "pokol"—hell, "stregoica"—witch, "vrolok" and "vlkoslak"—both of which mean the same thing, one being Slovak and the other Servian for something that is either were-wolf or vampire.
>
> When we started, the crowd round the inn door, which had by this time swelled to a considerable size, all made the sign of the cross and pointed two fingers towards me. With some difficulty I got a fellow-passenger to tell me what they meant; he wouldn't answer at first, but on learning that I was English, he explained that it was a charm or guard against the evil eye. This was not very pleasant for me, just starting for an unknown place to meet an unknown man; but everyone seemed so kind-hearted, and so sorrowful, and so sympathetic that I couldn't but be touched. I shall never forget the last glimpse which I had of the inn-yard and its crowd of picturesque figures, all crossing themselves, as they stood round the wide archway, with its background of rich foliage of oleander and orange trees in green tubs clustered in the centre of the yard. Then our driver cracked his big whip over his four small horses, which ran abreast, and we set off on our journey.
>
> I soon lost sight and recollection of ghostly fears in the beauty of the scene as we drove along, although had I known the language, or rather languages, which my fellow-passengers were speaking, I might not have been able to throw them off so easily. Before us lay a green sloping land full of forests and woods, with here and there steep hills, crowned with clumps of trees or with farmhouses, the blank gable end to the road. There was everywhere a bewildering mass of fruit blossom—apple, plum, pear, cherry; and as we drove by I could see the green grass under the trees spangled with the fallen petals. In and out amongst these green hills of what they call here the "Mittel Land" ran the road, losing itself as it swept round the grassy curve, or was shut out by the straggling ends of pine woods, which here and there ran down the hillsides like tongues of flame. The road was rugged, but still we seemed to fly over it with a feverish haste. I couldn't understand then what the haste meant, but the driver was evidently bent on losing no time in reaching Borgo Prund.

9. What type of narrator is found in this passage?
   a. First person
   b. Second person
   c. Third-person limited
   d. Third-person omniscient

10. Which of the following is true of the traveler?
    a. He wishes the driver would go faster.
    b. He's returning to the country of his birth.
    c. He has some familiarity with the local customs.
    d. He doesn't understand all of the languages being used.

11. How does the traveler's mood change between the second and third paragraphs?
    a. From relaxed to rushed
    b. From fearful to charmed
    c. From confused to enlightened
    d. From comfortable to exhausted

12. Who is the traveler going to meet?
    a. A kind landlady
    b. A distant relative
    c. A friendly villager
    d. A complete stranger

13. Based on the details in this passage, what can readers probably expect to happen in the story?
    a. The traveler will become a farmer.
    b. The traveler will arrive late at his destination.
    c. The traveler will soon encounter danger or evil.
    d. The traveler will have a pleasant journey and make many new friends.

14. Which sentence from the passage provides a clue for question 13?
    a. "I must say they weren't cheering to me, for amongst them were "Ordog"—Satan, "pokol"—hell, "stregoica"—witch, "vrolok" and "vlkoslak"—both of which mean the same thing, one being Slovak and the other Servian for something that is either were-wolf or vampire."
    b. "When I got on the coach the driver had not taken his seat, and I saw him talking with the landlady."
    c. "Then our driver cracked his big whip over his four small horses, which ran abreast, and we set off on our journey."
    d. "There was everywhere a bewildering mass of fruit blossom—apple, plum, pear, cherry; and as we drove by I could see the green grass under the trees spangled with the fallen petals."

Questions 15–23 are based on the following passages.

Passage I

Lethal force, or deadly force, is defined as the physical means to cause death or serious harm to another individual. The law holds that lethal force is only accepted when you or another person are in immediate and unavoidable danger of death or severe bodily harm. For example, a person could be beating a weaker person in such a way that they are suffering severe enough trauma that could result in death or serious harm. This would be an instance where lethal force would be acceptable and possibly the only way to save that person from irrevocable damage.

Another example of when to use lethal force would be when someone enters your home with a deadly weapon. The intruder's presence and possession of the weapon indicate mal-intent and the ability to inflict death or severe injury to you and your loved ones. Again, lethal force can be used in this situation. Lethal force can also be applied to prevent the harm of another individual.

If a woman is being brutally assaulted and is unable to fend off an attacker, lethal force can be used to defend her as a last-ditch effort. If she is in immediate jeopardy of rape, harm, and/or death, lethal force could be the only response that could effectively deter the assailant.

The key to understanding the concept of lethal force is the term *last resort*. Deadly force cannot be taken back; it should be used only to prevent severe harm or death. The law does distinguish whether the means of one's self-defense is fully warranted, or if the individual goes out of control in the process. If you continually attack the assailant after they are rendered incapacitated, this would be causing unnecessary harm, and the law can bring charges against you. Likewise, if you kill an attacker unnecessarily after defending yourself, you can be charged with murder. This would move lethal force beyond necessary defense, making it no longer a last resort but rather a use of excessive force.

Passage II

Assault is the unlawful attempt of one person to apply apprehension on another individual by an imminent threat or by initiating offensive contact. Assaults can vary, encompassing physical strikes, threatening body language, and even provocative language. In the case of the latter, even if a hand has not been laid, it is still considered an assault because of its threatening nature.

Let's look at an example: A homeowner is angered because his neighbor blows fallen leaves into his freshly mowed lawn. Irate, the homeowner gestures a fist to his fellow neighbor and threatens to bash his head in for littering on his lawn. The homeowner's physical motions and verbal threat heralds a physical threat against the other neighbor. These factors classify the homeowner's reaction as an assault. If the angry neighbor hits the threatening homeowner in retaliation, that would constitute an assault as well because he physically hit the homeowner.

Assault also centers on the involvement of weapons in a conflict. If someone fires a gun at another person, this could be interpreted as an assault unless the shooter acted in self-defense. If an individual drew a gun or a knife on someone with the intent to harm them, that would be considered assault. However, it's also considered an assault if someone simply aimed a weapon, loaded or not, at another person in a threatening manner.

15. What is the purpose of the second passage?
    a. Inform the reader about what assault is and how it is committed.
    b. Inform the reader about how assault is a minor example of lethal force.
    c. Disprove the previous passage concerning lethal force.
    d. The author is recounting an incident in which they were assaulted.

16. Which of the following situations, according to the passages, would not constitute an illegal use of lethal force?
    a. A disgruntled cashier yells obscenities at a customer.
    b. A thief is seen running away with stolen cash.
    c. A man is attacked in an alley by another man with a knife.
    d. A woman punches another woman in a bar.

17. Given the information in the passages, which of the following must be true about assault?

a. All assault is considered expression of lethal force.

b. There are various forms of assault.

c. Smaller, weaker people cannot commit assault.

d. Assault is justified only as a last resort.

18. Which of the following, if true, would most seriously undermine the explanation proposed by the author in Passage I, third paragraph?

a. An instance of lethal force in self-defense is not absolutely absolved from blame. The law takes into account the necessary use of force at the time it is committed.

b. An individual who uses necessary defense under lethal force is in direct compliance of the law under most circumstances.

c. Lethal force in self-defense should be forgiven in all cases for the peace of mind of the primary victim.

d. The use of lethal force is not evaluated on the intent of the user, but rather the severity of the primary attack that warranted self-defense.

19. Based on the passages, what can we infer about the relationship between assault and lethal force?

a. An act of lethal force always leads to a type of assault.

b. An assault will result in someone using lethal force.

c. An assault with deadly intent can lead to an individual using lethal force to preserve their well-being.

d. If someone uses self-defense in a conflict, this is called deadly force; if actions or threats are intended, it is called assault.

20. Which of the following best describes the way the passages are structured?

a. Both passages open by defining a legal concept and then continue to describe situations in order to further explain the concept.

b. Both passages begin with situations, introduce accepted definitions, and then cite legal ramifications.

c. Passage one presents a long definition while the second passage begins by showing an example of assault.

d. Both cite specific legal doctrines, then proceed to explain the rulings.

21. What can we infer about the role of intent in lethal force and assault?

a. Intent is very important for determining both lethal force and assault; intent is examined in both parties and helps determine the severity of the issue.

b. Intent is vital for determining the lawfulness of using lethal force.

c. Intent is only taken into account for assault charges.

d. The intent of the assailant is the main focus for determining legal ramifications; it is used to determine if the defender was justified in using force to respond.

22. The author uses the example in the second paragraph of Passage II in order to do what?
    a. To demonstrate two different types of assault by showing how each specifically relates to the other.
    b. To demonstrate a single example of two different types of assault, then adding in the third type of assault in the example's conclusion.
    c. To prove that the definition of lethal force is altered when the victim in question is a homeowner and his property is threatened.
    d. To suggest that verbal assault can be an exaggerated crime by the law and does not necessarily lead to physical violence.
    e. To demonstrate that threatening body language is only considered a type of assault if it leads to physical violence.

23. *Irrevocable* most nearly means which of the following?
    a. Temporary
    b. Irreversible
    c. Irrelevant
    d. Accidental

Questions 24–29 are based on the following passage:

> As long ago as 1860 it was the proper thing to be born at home. At present, so I am told, the high gods of medicine have decreed that the first cries of the young shall be uttered upon the anesthetic air of a hospital, preferably a fashionable one. So young Mr. and Mrs. Roger Button were fifty years ahead of style when they decided, one day in the summer of 1860, that their first baby should be born in a hospital. Whether this anachronism had any bearing upon the astonishing history I am about to set down will never be known.
>
> I shall tell you what occurred, and let you judge for yourself.
>
> The Roger Buttons held an enviable position, both social and financial, in ante-bellum Baltimore. They were related to the This Family and the That Family, which, as every Southerner knew, entitled them to membership in that enormous peerage which largely populated the Confederacy. This was their first experience with the charming old custom of having babies—Mr. Button was naturally nervous. He hoped it would be a boy so that he could be sent to Yale College in Connecticut, at which institution Mr. Button himself had been known for four years by the somewhat obvious nickname of "Cuff."
>
> On the September morning <u>consecrated</u> to the enormous event he arose nervously at six o'clock dressed himself, adjusted an impeccable stock, and hurried forth through the streets of Baltimore to the hospital, to determine whether the darkness of the night had borne in new life upon its bosom.
>
> When he was approximately a hundred yards from the Maryland Private Hospital for Ladies and Gentlemen he saw Doctor Keene, the family physician, descending the front steps, rubbing his hands together with a washing movement—as all doctors are required to do by the unwritten ethics of their profession.
>
> Mr. Roger Button, the president of Roger Button & Co., Wholesale Hardware, began to run toward Doctor Keene with much less dignity than was expected from a Southern gentleman of that picturesque period. "Doctor Keene!" he called. "Oh, Doctor Keene!"

The doctor heard him, faced around, and stood waiting, a curious expression settling on his harsh, medicinal face as Mr. Button drew near.

"What happened?" demanded Mr. Button, as he came up in a gasping rush. "What was it? How is she? A boy? Who is it? What—"

"Talk sense!" said Doctor Keene sharply. He appeared somewhat irritated.

"Is the child born?" begged Mr. Button.

Doctor Keene frowned. "Why, yes, I suppose so—after a fashion." Again he threw a curious glance at Mr. Button.

The Curious Case of Benjamin Button, F.S. Fitzgerald, 1922

24. What major event is about to happen in this story?
    a. Mr. Button is about to go to a funeral.
    b. Mr. Button's wife is about to have a baby.
    c. Mr. Button is getting ready to go to the doctor's office.
    d. Mr. Button is about to go shopping for new clothes.

25. What kind of tone does the above passage have?
    a. Nervous and Excited
    b. Sad and Angry
    c. Shameful and Confused
    d. Grateful and Joyous

26. What is the meaning of the word "consecrated" in paragraph 4?
    a. Numbed
    b. Chained
    c. Dedicated
    d. Moved

27. What does the author mean to do by adding the following statement?

    "rubbing his hands together with a washing movement—as all doctors are required to do by the unwritten ethics of their profession."

    a. Suggesting that Mr. Button is tired of the doctor.
    b. Trying to explain the detail of the doctor's profession.
    c. Hinting to readers that the doctor is an unethical man.
    d. Giving readers a visual picture of what the doctor is doing.

28. Which of the following best describes the development of this passage?
    a. It starts in the middle of a narrative in order to transition smoothly to a conclusion.
    b. It is a chronological narrative from beginning to end.
    c. The sequence of events is backwards—we go from future events to past events.
    d. To introduce the setting of the story and its characters.

29. Which of the following is an example of an imperative sentence?
    a. "Oh, Doctor Keene!"
    b. "Talk sense!"
    c. "Is the child born?"
    d. "Why, yes, I suppose so—"

Questions 30–37 are based on the following passage.

In the quest to understand existence, modern philosophers must question if humans can fully comprehend the world. Classical western approaches to philosophy tend to hold that one can understand something, be it an event or object, by standing outside of the phenomena and observing it. It is then by unbiased observation that one can grasp the details of the world. This seems to hold true for many things. Scientists conduct experiments and record their findings, and thus many natural phenomena become comprehendible. However, several of these observations were possible because humans used tools in order to make these discoveries.

This may seem like an extraneous matter. After all, people invented things like microscopes and telescopes in order to enhance their capacity to view cells or the movement of stars. While humans are still capable of seeing things, the question remains if human beings have the capacity to fully observe and see the world in order to understand it. It would not be an impossible stretch to argue that what humans see through a microscope is not the exact thing itself, but a human interpretation of it.

This would seem to be the case in the "Business of the Holes" experiment conducted by Richard Feynman. To study the way electrons behave, Feynman set up a barrier with two holes and a plate. The plate was there to indicate how many times the electrons would pass through the hole(s). Rather than casually observe the electrons acting under normal circumstances, Feynman discovered that electrons behave in two totally different ways depending on whether or not they are observed. The electrons that were observed had passed through either one of the holes or were caught on the plate as particles. However, electrons that weren't observed acted as waves instead of particles and passed through both holes. This indicated that electrons have a dual nature. Electrons seen by the human eye act like particles, while unseen electrons act like waves of energy.

This dual nature of the electrons presents a conundrum. While humans now have a better understanding of electrons, the fact remains that people cannot entirely perceive how electrons behave without the use of instruments. We can only observe one of the mentioned behaviors, which only provides a partial understanding of the entire function of electrons. Therefore, we're forced to ask ourselves whether the world we observe is objective or if it is subjectively perceived by humans. Or, an alternative question: can man understand the world only through machines that will allow them to observe natural phenomena?

Both questions humble man's capacity to grasp the world. However, those ideas don't take into account that many phenomena have been proven by human beings without the use of machines, such as the discovery of gravity. Like all philosophical questions, whether man's reason and observation alone can understand the universe can be approached from many angles.

30. The word *extraneous* in paragraph two can be best interpreted as referring to which of the following?

a. Indispensable
b. Bewildering
c. Fallacious
d. Exuberant
e. Superfluous

31. What is the author's motivation for writing the passage?

a. To bring to light an alternative view on human perception by examining the role of technology in human understanding.
b. To educate the reader on the latest astroparticle physics discovery and offer terms that may be unfamiliar to the reader.
c. To argue that humans are totally blind to the realities of the world by presenting an experiment that proves that electrons are not what they seem on the surface.
d. To reflect on opposing views of human understanding.
e. To disprove classical philosophy by comparing more accurate technology to the speculations of the ancient philosophers.

32. Which of the following most closely resembles the way in which paragraph four is structured?

a. It offers one solution, questions the solution, and then ends with an alternative solution.
b. It presents an inquiry, explains the detail of that inquiry, and then offers a solution.
c. It presents a problem, explains the details of that problem, and then ends with more inquiry.
d. It gives a definition, offers an explanation, and then ends with an inquiry.
e. It presents a problem, offers an example, and then ends with a solution.

33. For the classical approach to understanding to hold true, which of the following must be required?

a. A telescope.
b. A recording device.
c. Multiple witnesses present.
d. The person observing must be unbiased.
e. The person observing must prove their theory beyond a doubt.

34. Which best describes how the electrons in the experiment behaved like waves?

a. The electrons moved up and down like actual waves.
b. The electrons passed through both holes and then onto the plate.
c. The electrons converted to photons upon touching the plate.
d. The electrons were seen passing through one hole or the other.
e. The electrons were glowing during the experiment, indicating light waves were moving them.

35. The author mentions "gravity" in the last paragraph in order to do what?

a. In order to show that different natural phenomena test man's ability to grasp the world.
b. To prove that since man has not measured it with the use of tools or machines, humans cannot know the true nature of gravity.
c. To demonstrate an example of natural phenomena humans discovered and understand without the use of tools or machines.
d. To show an alternative solution to the nature of electrons that humans have not thought of yet.
e. To look toward the future of technology so that we may understand the dual nature of all phenomena, including gravity.

36. Which situation best parallels the revelation of the dual nature of electrons discovered in Feynman's experiment?

a. Ancient Greeks believed that Zeus hurled lightning down to Earth. In reality, lightning is caused by supercharged electrons, and happens either inside the clouds or between the cloud and the ground.
b. The coelacanth was thought to be extinct, but a live specimen was just recently discovered. There are now two living species of coelacanth known to man, and both are believed to be endangered.
c. In the Middle Ages, blacksmiths added carbon to iron, thus inventing steel. The consequences of this important discovery would have its biggest effects during the industrial revolution.
d. In order to better examine and treat broken bones, the x-ray machine was invented and put to use in hospitals and medical centers.
e. A man is born color-blind and grows up observing everything in lighter or darker shades. With the invention of special goggles he puts on, he discovers that there are other colors in addition to different shades.

37. Which statement about technology would the author likely disagree with?

a. Technology can help expand the field of human vision.
b. Technology renders human observation irrelevant.
c. Developing tools used in observation and research indicates growing understanding of our world in itself.
d. Studying certain phenomena necessitates the use of tools and machines.
e. Classical observation still serves a function in our world.

Questions 38–42 are based on the following passage.

The Middle Ages were a time of great superstition and theological debate. Many beliefs were developed and practiced, while some died out or were listed as heresy. Boethianism is a Medieval theological philosophy that attributes sin to gratification and righteousness with virtue and God's providence. Boethianism holds that sin, greed, and corruption are means to attain temporary pleasure, but that they inherently harm the person's soul as well as other human beings.

In *The Canterbury Tales,* we observe more instances of bad actions punished than goodness being rewarded. This would appear to be some reflection of Boethianism. In the "Pardoner's Tale," all three thieves wind up dead, which is a result of their desire for wealth. Each wrong doer pays with their life, and they are unable to enjoy the wealth they worked to steal. Within his tales, Chaucer gives reprieve to people undergoing struggle, but also interweaves stories of contemptible individuals being cosmically punished for their wickedness. The thieves idolize physical wealth, which leads to their downfall. This same theme and ideological principle of Boethianism is repeated in the "Friar's Tale," whose summoner character attempts to gain further wealth by partnering with a demon. The summoner's refusal to repent for his avarice and corruption leads to the demon dragging his soul to Hell. Again, we see the theme of the individual who puts faith and morality aside in favor for a physical prize. The result, of course, is that the summoner loses everything.

The examples of the righteous being rewarded tend to appear in a spiritual context within the *Canterbury Tales*. However, there are a few instances where we see goodness resulting in physical reward. In the Prioress' Tale, we see corporal punishment for barbarism *and* a reward for goodness. The Jews are punished for their murder of the child, giving a sense of law and order (though racist) to the plot. While the boy does die, he is granted a lasting reward by being able to sing even after his death, a miracle that marks that the murdered youth led a pure life. Here, the miracle represents eternal favor with God.

Again, we see the theological philosophy of Boethianism in Chaucer's *The Canterbury Tales* through acts of sin and righteousness and the consequences that follow. When pleasures of the world are sought instead of God's favor, we see characters being punished in tragic ways. However, the absence of worldly lust has its own set of consequences for the characters seeking to obtain God's favor.

38. What would be a potential reward for living a good life, as described in Boethianism?
   a. A long life sustained by the good deeds one has done over a lifetime.
   b. Wealth and fertility for oneself and the extension of one's family line.
   c. Vengeance for those who have been persecuted by others who have a capacity for committing wrongdoing.
   d. The act of reaching Sainthood.
   e. God's divine favor for one's righteousness.

39. What might be the main reason why the author chose to discuss Boethianism through examining *The Canterbury Tales*?
   a. *The Canterbury Tales* is a well-known text.
   b. *The Canterbury Tales* is the only known fictional text that contains use of Boethianism.
   c. *The Canterbury Tales* presents a manuscript written in the medieval period that can help illustrate Boethianism through stories and show how people of the time might have responded to the idea.
   d. Within each individual tale in *The Canterbury Tales*, the reader has the opportunity to read about different levels of Boethianism and how each level leads to greater enlightenment.
   e. Chaucer, who wrote *The Canterbury Tales,* was a devoted Boethianist.

40. What "ideological principle" is the author referring to in the middle of the second paragraph when talking about the "Friar's Tale"?
   a. The principle that the act of ravaging another's possessions is the same as ravaging one's soul.
   b. The principle that thieves who idolize physical wealth will be punished in an earthly sense as well as eternally.
   c. The principle that fraternization with a demon will result in one losing everything, including their life.
   d. The principle that a desire for material goods leads to moral malfeasance punishable by a higher being.
   e. The principle that wealth is impossible to enjoy when one has been corrupted in the pursuit of it.

41. Which of the following words, if substituted for the word *avarice* in paragraph two, would LEAST change the meaning of the sentence?

a. Perniciousness
b. Pithiness
c. Parsimoniousness
d. Pompousness
e. Precariousness

42. Based on the passage, what view does Boethianism take on desire?

a. Desire does not exist in the context of Boethianism.
b. Desire is a virtue and should be welcomed.
c. Having desire is evidence of demonic possession.
d. Desire for pleasure can lead toward sin.
e. Desire is the result of original sin.

Questions 46–51 are based upon the following passage from "Common Sense" by Thomas Paine:

"MANKIND being originally equals in the order of creation, the equality could only be destroyed by some subsequent circumstance; the distinctions of rich, and poor, may in a great measure be accounted for, and that without having recourse to the harsh ill sounding names of oppression and avarice. Oppression is often the consequence, but seldom or never the means of riches; and though avarice will preserve a man from being necessitously poor, it generally makes him too timorous to be wealthy.

But there is another and greater distinction for which no truly natural or religious reason can be assigned, and that is, the distinction of men into KINGS and SUBJECTS. Male and female are the distinctions of nature, good and bad the distinctions of heaven; but how a race of men came into the world so exalted above the rest, and distinguished like some new species, is worth enquiring into, and whether they are the means of happiness or of misery to mankind.

In the early ages of the world, according to the scripture chronology, there were no kings; the consequence of which was there were no wars; it is the pride of kings which throw mankind into confusion Holland without a king hath enjoyed more peace for this last century than any of the monarchical governments in Europe. Antiquity favors the same remark; for the quiet and rural lives of the first patriarchs hath a happy something in them, which vanishes away when we come to the history of Jewish royalty.

Government by kings was first introduced into the world by the Heathens, from whom the children of Israel copied the custom. It was the most prosperous invention the Devil ever set on foot for the promotion of idolatry. The Heathens paid divine honors to their deceased kings, and the Christian world hath improved on the plan by doing the same to their living ones. How impious is the title of sacred majesty applied to a worm, who in the midst of his splendor is crumbling into dust!

As the exalting one man so greatly above the rest cannot be justified on the equal rights of nature, so neither can it be defended on the authority of scripture; for the will of the Almighty, as declared by Gideon and the prophet Samuel, expressly disapproves of government by kings. All anti-monarchical parts of scripture have been very smoothly glossed over in monarchical governments, but they undoubtedly merit the attention of countries, which have their governments yet to form. "Render unto Caesar the things which are Caesar's" is the scripture doctrine of courts, yet it is no support of monarchical government, for the Jews at that time were without a king, and in a state of vassalage to the Romans.

Near three thousand years passed away from the Mosaic account of the creation, till the Jews under a national delusion requested a king. Till then their form of government (except in extraordinary cases, where the Almighty interposed) was a kind of republic administered by a judge and the elders of the tribes. Kings they had none, and it was held sinful to acknowledge any being under that title but the Lord of Hosts. And when a man seriously reflects on the idolatrous homage which is paid to the persons of Kings, he need not wonder, that the Almighty ever jealous of his honor, should disapprove of a form of government which so impiously invades the prerogative of heaven.

43. According to passage, what role does avarice, or greed, play in poverty?
    a. It can make a man very wealthy
    b. It is the consequence of wealth
    c. Avarice can prevent a man from being poor, but too fearful to be very wealthy
    d. Avarice is what drives a person to be very wealthy

44. Of these distinctions, which does the author believe to be beyond natural or religious reason?
    a. Good and bad
    b. Male and female
    c. Human and animal
    d. King and subjects

45. According to the passage, what are the Heathens responsible for?
    a. Government by kings
    b. Quiet and rural lives of patriarchs
    c. Paying divine honors to their living kings
    d. Equal rights of nature

46. Which of the following best states Paine's rationale for the denouncement of monarchy?
    a. It is against the laws of nature
    b. It is against the equal rights of nature and is denounced in scripture
    c. Despite scripture, a monarchal government is unlawful
    d. Neither the law nor scripture denounce monarchy

47. Based on the passage, what is the best definition of the word *idolatrous*?
    a. Worshipping heroes
    b. Being deceitful
    c. Sinfulness
    d. Engaging in illegal activities

48. What is the essential meaning of lines 41-44?

> And when a man seriously reflects on the idolatrous homage which is paid to the persons of Kings, he need not wonder, that the Almighty ever jealous of his honor, should disapprove of a form of government which so impiously invades the prerogative of heaven.

a. God would disapprove of the irreverence of a monarchical government.
b. With careful reflection, men should realize that heaven is not promised.
c. God will punish those that follow a monarchical government.
d. Belief in a monarchical government cannot coexist with belief in God.

Questions 49–52 refer to the following passage.

> Although many Missourians know that Harry S. Truman and Walt Disney hailed from their great state, probably far fewer know that it was also home to the remarkable George Washington Carver. At the end of the Civil War, Moses Carver, the slave owner who owned George's parents, decided to keep George and his brother and raise them on his farm. As a child, George was driven to learn and he loved painting. He even went on to study art while in college but was encouraged to pursue botany instead. He spent much of his life helping others by showing them better ways to farm; his ideas improved agricultural productivity in many countries. One of his most notable contributions to the newly emerging class of Negro farmers was to teach them the negative effects of agricultural monoculture, i.e. growing the same crops in the same fields year after year, depleting the soil of much needed nutrients and resulting in a lesser yielding crop. Carver was an innovator, always thinking of new and better ways to do things, and is most famous for his over three hundred uses for the peanut. Toward the end of his career, Carver returned to his first love of art. Through his artwork, he hoped to inspire people to see the beauty around them and to do great things themselves. When Carver died, he left his money to help fund ongoing agricultural research. Today, people still visit and study at the George Washington Carver Foundation at Tuskegee Institute.

49. Which of the following describes the kind of writing used in the above passage?
a. Narrative
b. Persuasive
c. Technical
d. Expository

50. According to the passage, what was George Washington Carver's first love?
a. Plants
b. Art
c. Animals
d. Soil

51. According to the passage, what is the best definition for agricultural monoculture?
a. The practice of producing or growing a single crop or plant species over a wide area and for a large number of consecutive years
b. The practice of growing a diversity of crops and rotating them from year to year
c. The practice of growing crops organically to avoid the use of pesticides
d. The practice of charging an inflated price for cheap crops to obtain a greater profit margin

52. Which of the following is the best summary of this passage?

a. George Washington Carver was born at a time when scientific discovery was at a virtual standstill.

b. Because he was African American, there were not many opportunities for George Washington Carver.

c. George Washington Carver was an intelligent man whose research and discoveries had an impact worldwide.

d. George Washington Carver was far more successful as an artist than he was as a scientist.

Writing and Language Test

Read the selection about travelling in an RV and answer Questions 1–7.

I have to admit that when my father bought a recreational vehicle (RV), I thought he was making a huge mistake. I didn't really know anything about RVs, but I knew that my dad was as big a "city slicker" as there was. (1) <u>In fact, I even thought he might have gone a little bit crazy.</u> On trips to the beach, he preferred to swim at the pool, and whenever he went hiking, he avoided touching any plants for fear that they might be poison ivy. Why would this man, with an almost irrational fear of the outdoors, want a 40-foot camping behemoth?

(2) <u>The RV</u> was a great purchase for our family and brought us all closer together. Every morning (3) <u>we would wake up, eat breakfast, and broke camp.</u> We laughed at our own comical attempts to back The Beast into spaces that seemed impossibly small. (4) <u>We rejoiced as "hackers."</u> When things inevitably went wrong and we couldn't solve the problems on our own, we discovered the incredible helpfulness and friendliness of the RV community. (5) <u>We even made some new friends in the process.</u>

(6) <u>Above all, it allowed us to share adventures. While travelling across America</u>, which we could not have experienced in cars and hotels. Enjoying a campfire on a chilly summer evening with the mountains of Glacier National Park in the background, or waking up early in the morning to see the sun rising over the distant spires of Arches National Park are memories that will always stay with me and our entire family. (7) <u>Those are also memories that my siblings and me</u> have now shared with our own children.

1. Which of the following would be the best choice for this sentence (reproduced below)?

   In fact, I even thought he might have gone a little bit crazy.

   a. (No change; best as written.)
   b. Move the sentence so that it comes before the preceding sentence.
   c. Move the sentence to the end of the first paragraph.
   d. Omit the sentence.

2. In context, which is the best version of the underlined portion of this sentence (reproduced below)?

   <u>The RV</u> was a great purchase for our family and brought us all closer together.

   a. NO CHANGE
   b. Not surprisingly, the RV
   c. Furthermore, the RV
   d. As it turns out, the RV

3. Which is the best version of the underlined portion of this sentence (reproduced below)?

Every morning we would wake up, eat breakfast, and broke camp.

a. NO CHANGE
b. we would wake up, eat breakfast, and break camp.
c. would we wake up, eat breakfast, and break camp?
d. we are waking up, eating breakfast, and breaking camp.

4. Which is the best version of the underlined portion of this sentence (reproduced below)?

We rejoiced as "hackers."

a. NO CHANGE
b. To a nagging problem of technology, we rejoiced as "hackers."
c. We rejoiced when we figured out how to "hack" a solution to a nagging technological problem.
d. To "hack" our way to a solution, we had to rejoice.

5. Which is the best version of the underlined portion of this sentence (reproduced below)?

We even made some new friends in the process.

a. NO CHANGE
b. In the process was the friends we were making.
c. We are even making some new friends in the process.
d. We will make new friends in the process.

6. Which is the best version of the underlined portion of this sentence (reproduced below)?

Above all, it allowed us to share adventures. While travelling across America, which we could not have experienced in cars and hotels.

a. NO CHANGE
b. Above all, it allowed us to share adventures while traveling across America
c. Above all, it allowed us to share adventures; while traveling across America
d. Above all, it allowed us to share adventures—while traveling across America

7. Which is the best version of the underlined portion of this sentence (reproduced below)?

Those are also memories that my siblings and me have now shared with our own children.

a. NO CHANGE
b. Those are also memories that me and my siblings
c. Those are also memories that my siblings and I
d. Those are also memories that I and my siblings

Read the essay entitled "Education is Essential to Civilization" and answer Questions 8–22.

Early in my career, (21) a master's teacher shared this thought with me "Education is the last bastion of civility." While I did not completely understand the scope of those words at the time, I have since come to realize the depth, breadth, truth, and significance of what he said. (22) Education provides society with a vehicle for (23) raising it's children to be civil, decent, human beings with something valuable to contribute to the world. It is really what makes us human and what (24) distinguishes us as civilised creatures.

Being "civilized" humans means being "whole" humans. Education must address the mind, body, and soul of students. (25) It would be detrimental to society, only meeting the needs of the mind, if our schools were myopic in their focus. As humans, we are multi-dimensional, multi-faceted beings who need more than head knowledge to survive. (26) The human heart and psyche have to be fed in order for the mind to develop properly, and the body must be maintained and exercised to help fuel the working of the brain. Education is a basic human right, and it allows us to sustain a democratic society in which participation is fundamental to its success. It should inspire students to seek better solutions to world problems and to dream of a more equitable society. Education should never discriminate on any basis, and it should create individuals who are self-sufficient, patriotic, and tolerant of (27) others' ideas.

(28) All children can learn. Although not all children learn in the same manner. All children learn best, however, when their basic physical needs are met and they feel safe, secure, and loved. Students are much more responsive to a teacher who values them and shows them respect as individual people. Teachers must model at all times the way they expect students to treat them and their peers. If teachers set high expectations for (29) there students, the students will rise to that high level. Teachers must make the well-being of students their primary focus and must not be afraid to let students learn from their own mistakes.

In the modern age of technology, a teacher's focus is no longer the "what" of the content, (30) but more importantly, the 'why.' Students are bombarded with information and have access to ANY information they need right at their fingertips. Teachers have to work harder than ever before to help students identify salient information (31) so to think critically about the information they encounter. Students have to (32) read between the lines, identify bias, and determine who they can trust in the milieu of ads, data, and texts presented to them.

Schools must work in consort with families in this important mission. While children spend most of their time in school, they are dramatically and indelibly shaped (33) with the influences of their family and culture. Teachers must not only respect this fact, (34) but must strive to include parents in the education of their children and must work to keep parents informed of progress and problems. Communication between classroom and home is essential for a child's success.

Humans have always aspired to be more, do more, and to better ourselves and our communities. This is where education lies, right at the heart of humanity's desire to be all that we can be. Education helps us strive for higher goals and better treatment of ourselves and others. I shudder to think what would become of us if education ceased to be the "last bastion of civility." (35) We must be unapologetic about expecting excellence from our students? Our very existence depends upon it.

8. Which is the best version of the underlined portion of this sentence (reproduced below)?

Early in my career, <u>a master's teacher shared this thought with me "Education is the last bastion of civility."</u>

a. NO CHANGE
b. a master's teacher shared this thought with me: "Education is the last bastion of civility."
c. a master's teacher shared this thought with me: "Education is the last bastion of civility".
d. a master's teacher shared this thought with me. "Education is the last bastion of civility."

9. Which is the best version of the underlined portion of this sentence (reproduced below)?

<u>Education provides</u> society with a vehicle

a. NO CHANGE
b. Education provide
c. Education will provide
d. Education providing

10. Which is the best version of the underlined portion of this sentence (reproduced below)?

for <u>raising it's children to be</u> civil, decent, human beings with something valuable to contribute to the world.

a. NO CHANGE
b. raises its children to be
c. raising its' children to be
d. raising its children to be

11. Which of these, if any, is misspelled?

It is really what makes us human and what <u>distinguishes</u> us as <u>civilised</u> <u>creatures.</u>

a. NO CHANGE
b. distinguishes
c. civilised
d. creatures

12. Which is the best version of the underlined portion of this sentence (reproduced below)?

It would be detrimental to society, only meeting the needs of the mind, if our schools were myopic in their focus.

a. NO CHANGE
b. It would be detrimental to society if our schools were myopic in their focus, only meeting the needs of the mind.
c. Only meeting the needs of our mind, our schools were myopic in their focus, detrimental to society.
d. Myopic is the focus of our schools, being detrimental to society for only meeting the needs of the mind.

13. Which of these sentences, if any, should begin a new paragraph?

The human heart and psyche have to be fed in order for the mind to develop properly, and the body must be maintained and exercised to help fuel the working of the brain. Education is a basic human right, and it allows us to sustain a democratic society in which participation is fundamental to its success. It should inspire students to seek better solutions to world problems and to dream of a more equitable society.

a. NO CHANGE
b. The human heart and psyche have to be fed in order for the mind to develop properly, and the body must be maintained and exercised to help fuel the working of the brain.
c. Education is a basic human right, and it allows us to sustain a democratic society in which participation is fundamental to its success.
d. It should inspire students to seek better solutions to world problems and to dream of a more equitable society.

14. Which is the best version of the underlined portion of this sentence (reproduced below)?

Education should never discriminate on any basis, and it should create individuals who are self-sufficient, patriotic, and tolerant of others' ideas.

a. NO CHANGE
b. other's ideas
c. others ideas
d. others's ideas

15. Which is the best version of the underlined portion of this sentence (reproduced below)?

All children can learn. Although not all children learn in the same manner.

a. NO CHANGE
b. All children can learn although not all children learn in the same manner.
c. All children can learn although, not all children learn in the same manner.
d. All children can learn, although not all children learn in the same manner.

16. Which is the best version of the underlined portion of this sentence (reproduced below)?

If teachers set high expectations for there students, the students will rise to that high level.

a. NO CHANGE
b. they're students
c. their students
d. thare students

17. Which is the best version of the underlined portion of this sentence (reproduced below)?

In the modern age of technology, a teacher's focus is no longer the "what" of the content, but more importantly, the 'why.'

a. NO CHANGE
b. but more importantly, the "why."
c. but more importantly, the 'why'.
d. but more importantly, the "why".

18. Which is the best version of the underlined portion of this sentence (reproduced below)?

Teachers have to work harder than ever before to help students identify salient information so to think critically about the information they encounter.

a. NO CHANGE
b. and to think critically
c. but to think critically
d. nor to think critically

19. Which is the best version of the underlined portion of this sentence (reproduced below)?

Students have to read between the lines, identify bias, and determine who they can trust in the milieu of ads, data, and texts presented to them.

a. NO CHANGE
b. read between the lines, identify bias, and determining
c. read between the lines, identifying bias, and determining
d. reads between the lines, identifies bias, and determines

20. Which is the best version of the underlined portion of this sentence (reproduced below)?

While children spend most of their time in school, they are dramatically and indelibly shaped with the influences of their family and culture.

a. NO CHANGE
b. for the influences
c. to the influences
d. by the influences

21. Which is the best version of the underlined portion of this sentence (reproduced below)?

Teachers must not only respect this fact, but must strive to include parents in the education of their children and must work to keep parents informed of progress and problems.

a. NO CHANGE
b. but to strive
c. but striving
d. but strived

22. Which is the best version of the underlined portion of this sentence (reproduced below)?

We must be unapologetic about expecting excellence from our students? Our very existence depends upon it.

a. NO CHANGE
b. We must be unapologetic about expecting excellence from our students, our very existence depends upon it.
c. We must be unapologetic about expecting excellence from our students—our very existence depends upon it.
d. We must be unapologetic about expecting excellence from our students our very existence depends upon it.

Distrust in the Odyssey

In *The Odyssey*, Odysseus develops out of his experiences and the people he meets along his journey home. Many of his encounters involve female characters, some of whom offer Odysseus aid in his journey. (62) However, several of these characters deceive and even pose great danger to the hero. (63) This makes his journey home harder, it forces Odysseus himself to change and adapt in order to deal with the challenges. By the time Odysseus reaches home, he has become notably distrustful of women and even those who have true intentions. It is this sense of caution that ultimately serves Odysseus in successfully defeating the suitors of Penelope upon his return home.

Odysseus would not have been able to defeat the suitors without stealth and deception. He had (65) to conceal himself in order to achieve revenge. This is something we see earlier in Odysseus' encounter with Polyphemus the Cyclops. While not female, Polyphemus displayed feminine qualities characterized by his 'womb-like cave'. (66) Entering into the dwelling Odysseus directly demanded hospitality- Polyphemus instead butchered his men in spite of custom. In order to survive the encounter, Odysseus (67) relinquishes his true identity by telling Polyphemus his name is 'Nobody'. After the carnage of his men, he does not entrust the Cyclops with his true name. Rather, Odysseus uses disguise and cunning to trick Polyphemus into reopening the cave. When he emerges he is then reborn again as Odysseus.

This pattern is echoed again when Odysseus reaches Ithaca: "I look for endless ground to be spattered by the blood and brains of the suitors, these men who are eating all your substance away. But come now, let me make you so that no mortal can recognize you." (13: 394-397) Here Athena reveals her plan to disguise Odysseus as he makes his move against the suitors. Why do this? Why would Odysseus embrace the idea? With Polyphemus, Odysseus entered the cave trusting he would be received as a welcomed guest, but he wasn't. (68) Clearly, Odysseus isn't making the same mistake twice in trusting people to automatically abide by custom. Using a disguise allowed Odysseus to apply strategy in a similar manner he had with Polyphemus. This passage specifically describes the suitors as eating away at Odysseus' substance, seeming to further the parallel with Polyphemus who devoured Odysseus' men. (70) Also like with Polyphemus, Odysseus only reveals his true identity when he knows his plan has succeeded. The disguise concept presents a strategic role, but it also sheds further light on the impact of Odysseus' travels. To conceal (71) ones identity is to withhold trust.

The Circe episode matches Odysseus against someone he already knows to be untrustworthy. It is known that Circe welcomes all men who (72) enter upon her island with food and drink, but this is a deception meant to ensnare them. This xenia, or hospitality, that Odysseus would have been accustomed to, turns out to be farce. She violates the trust of her guests by turning them into swine, thus making her a deceitful host- and specifically- a woman Odysseus cannot trust. In order to (73) assure his and the crew's safety, Odysseus must look past her empty courtesy and deceive her in a way that will remedy the situation. With the knowledge of Circe's dark intentions (and Hermes' instructions), Odysseus attempts to out-maneuver Circe by making her think he will kill her (10: 321-323). By doing this he is taking on deceitful qualities so as to ensure he can bend her to proper behavior, which works. Still untrusting of Circe's submission though, Odysseus makes her swear a formal oath: "I would not be willing to go to bed with you unless you can bring yourself, O goddess, to swear me a great oath that there is no other evil hurt you devise against me." (10:342-344) Even though Odysseus tamed Circe, he is still distrustful. The 'great' oath becomes a final assurance that she is sincere. Until he knows for certain that no more treachery can befall him (the oath), he does not partake in showing any form of trust.

In the Land of the Dead, Odysseus encounters Agamemnon, who describes his own murder at the hand of his wife, Klytaimestra. Not only is this an example of a wife's betrayal, but a betrayal that appears close to Odysseus' own situation. (74) Like Agamemnon, Odysseus is returning home to his wife. However, Agamemnon didn't realize his wife had foul intentions, he trusted her to receive him with open arms:

"See, I had been thinking that I would be welcome to my children and thralls of my household when I came home, but she with thoughts surpassing grisly splashed the shame on herself and on the rest of her sex, on women still to come, even on the one whose acts are virtuous." (11: 430-434)

Clearly this is a cautionary story for Odysseus. After telling Odysseus of Klytaimestra's betrayal, Agamemnon warns Odysseus that all women are inherently distrustful. Now by this time Odysseus has already been deceived and nearly killed by female/female-like characters. Agamemnon's logic seems to back up what he already experienced. (75) As the text progresses, Odysseus encounters the Sirens and Calypso, who seem to corroborate the idea that women are bad news. However, what is most impressionable on Odysseus is Agamemnon's distrust of even virtuous women, "even on the one whose acts are virtuous". Who is to say that they cannot turn against him like Klytaimestra did against Agamemnon. This seems to cement in Odysseus a fear of betrayal, being welcomed in, just to be hurt.

23. What is the primary purpose of the passage?
    a. Inform the audience about the perils of Odysseus
    b. Argue that the Odyssey is a sexist text
    c. Prove that Odysseus' distrust of women was developed by past experiences which ultimately aided him in returning home
    d. Argue that femme-fatales were a key archetype in Ancient Greek literature

24.
    a. NO CHANGE
    b. However these
    c. However several of these
    d. Several of these

25.
    a. NO CHANGE
    b. This makes his journey home harder it forces Odysseus himself to change and adapt
    c. This makes his journey home harder which forces Odysseus to change and adapt
    d. This makes his journey home harder, forcing Odysseus to change and adapt

26. What function do the quotations provide in the passage?
    a. The quotes from *The Odyssey* help illustrate what the author is talking about
    b. The author provides these quotes to show where he gained his views on the text
    c. The quotes provide textual evidence to back up the writer's views
    d. All of the above are correct

27.
    a. NO CHANGE
    b. To be concealed
    c. Concealed
    d. Concealing

28. The author is trying to revise this sentence. He also wants to make it clear that Polyphemus' lack of hospitality violated Ancient Greek custom. Which of the following would be the best revision of this sentence?
    a. Odysseus directly entering into the dwelling and demanded hospitality – Polyphemus instead butchered his men in spite of custom.
    b. Odysseus entered Polyphemus' dwelling expecting to be received with customary hospitality, but instead, his men were butchered.
    c. Odysseus expected Polyphemus to receive him with hospitality, but instead, his men were butchered in gross opposition of what the custom demands.
    d. Polyphemus butchered Odysseus' men without any regard to hospitality.

29.
    a. NO CHANGE
    b. Conceals
    c. Withholds
    d. Surrenders

30.

a. NO CHANGE

b. Clearly Odysseus isn't making the same mistake twice in trusting people to automatically abide by custom.

c. Clearly, Odysseus isn't making the same mistake twice; trusting people to automatically abide by custom.

d. Odysseus isn't making the same mistake twice in trusting people, clearly, to automatically abide by custom.

31. Which statement would the author most likely use to describe Odysseus?

a. Odysseus' naturally cautious nature proved an important asset for him in the Odyssey

b. Odysseus is the noblest king of Ithaca

c. Odysseus' guile is his greatest asset

d. Odysseus has been molded by his journey to be naturally suspect of women and conventional situations

32.

a. NO CHANGE

b. As he did with Polyphemus

c. As he did before

d. With the exact method as he had with Polyphemus

33.

a. NO CHANGE

b. One's

c. Someone's

d. Oneself

34.

a. NO CHANGE

b. Land upon

c. Arrive on

d. Crash on

35.

a. NO CHANGE

b. Ensure

c. Prevent

d. Vindicate

36. The author is contemplating eliminating this sentence from the passage. Should he or should he not keep it within the text?

a. Remove the sentence; it merely repeats the one before it

b. Keep the sentence because it clarifies Agamemnon's and Odysseus' connection

c. Keep the sentence because it helps transition into the next sentence and the quote after that

d. Remove the sentence because the information is irrelevant

37.

a. NO CHANGE
b. As the text progresses Odysseus
c. The text progresses with Odysseus
d. As Odysseus progresses in the text

Read the following passage and answer Questions 38–44.

(41) Christopher Columbus is often credited for discovering America. This is incorrect. First, it is impossible to "discover" something where people already live; however, Christopher Columbus did explore places in the New World that were previously untouched by Europe, (42) so the ships set sail from Palos, Spain. Another correction must be made, as well: Christopher Columbus was not the first European explorer to reach the present day Americas! (43) Nevertheless, it was Leif Erikson who first came to the New World and contacted the natives, nearly five hundred years before Christopher Columbus.

Leif Erikson, the son of Erik the Red (a famous Viking outlaw and explorer in his own right), was born in either (44) 970 or 980. Depending on which historian you seek. (45) His own family, though, did not raise Leif, which was a Viking tradition. Instead, one of Erik's prisoners taught Leif reading and writing, languages, sailing, and weaponry. At age 12, Leif was considered a man and returned to his family. He killed a man during a dispute shortly after his return, and the council banished the Erikson clan to Greenland.

In 999, Leif left Greenland and traveled to Norway where he would serve as a guard to King Olaf Tryggvason. It was there that he became a convert to Christianity. (46) Later trying to return home, Leif with the intention of taking supplies and spreading Christianity to Greenland, however his ship was blown off course and he arrived in a strange new land: present day Newfoundland, Canada.

When he finally returned to his adopted homeland, Greenland, (47) Leif consults with a merchant who had also seen the shores of this previously unknown land we now know as Canada. The son of the legendary Viking explorer then gathered a crew of 35 men and set sail. Leif became the first European to touch foot in the New World as he explored present-day Baffin Island and Labrador, Canada. His crew called the land Vinland since it was plentiful with grapes.

During their time in present-day Newfoundland, Leif's expedition made contact with the natives whom they referred to as Skraelings (48) (which translates to 'wretched ones' in Norse). There are several secondhand accounts of their meetings. Some contemporaries described trade between the peoples. (49) Other accounts describes clashes where the Skraelings defeated the Viking explorers with long spears, while still others claim the Vikings dominated the natives. Regardless of the circumstances, it seems that the Vikings made contact of some kind. This happened around 1000, nearly five hundred years before Columbus famously sailed the ocean blue.

Eventually, in 1003, Leif set sail for home and arrived at Greenland with a ship full of timber. (50) In 1020, seventeen years later. The legendary Viking died. Many believe that Leif Erikson should receive more credit for his contributions in exploring the New World.

38. Which is the best version of the underlined portion of this sentence (reproduced below)?

Christopher Columbus is often credited for discovering America. This is incorrect.

a. NO CHANGE
b. Christopher Columbus is often credited for discovering America this is incorrect.
c. Christopher Columbus is often credited for discovering America, this is incorrect.
d. Christopher Columbus is often credited for discovering America: this is incorrect.

39. Which of the following facts would be the most relevant to include here?

however, Christopher Columbus did explore places in the New World that were previously untouched by Europe, so the ships set sail from Palos, Spain.

a. NO CHANGE
b. so Columbus discovered Watling Island in the Bahamas.
c. so the ships were named them the Santa María, the Pinta, and the Niña.
d. so the term "explorer" would be more accurate.

40. Which is the best version of the underlined portion of this sentence (reproduced below)?

Nevertheless, it was Leif Erikson who first came to the New World and contacted the natives, nearly five hundred years before Christopher Columbus.

a. NO CHANGE
b. Rather,
c. Finally,
d. Suddenly,

41. Which is the best version of the underlined portion of this sentence (reproduced below)?

Leif Erikson, the son of Erik the Red (a famous Viking outlaw and explorer in his own right), was born in either 970 or 980. Depending on which historian you seek.

a. NO CHANGE
b. 970 or 980! depending on which historian you seek.
c. 970 or 980, depending on which historian you seek.
d. 970 or 980; depending on which historian you seek.

42. Which of the following would be the best choice for this sentence?

His own family, though, did not raise Leif, which was a Viking tradition.

a. NO CHANGE
b. Move to the end of the second paragraph.
c. Move to the beginning of the second paragraph.
d. Switch with the following sentence.

43. Which is the best version of the underlined portion of this sentence (reproduced below)?

<u>Later trying to return home, Leif</u> with the intention of taking supplies and spreading Christianity to Greenland, however his ship was blown off course and he arrived in a strange new land: present day Newfoundland, Canada.

a. NO CHANGE
b. To return home later, Leif
c. Leif later tried to return home
d. Leif to return home tried later

44. Which is the best version of the underlined portion of this sentence (reproduced below)?

When he finally returned to his adopted homeland, Greenland, <u>Leif consults</u> with a merchant who had also seen the shores of this previously unknown land we now know as Canada.

a. NO CHANGE
b. Leif consulted
c. Leif consulting
d. Leif was consulted

Essay Prompt #2

As you read the essay below, consider how the author uses these following things:

- Evidence to support claims, like facts or examples
- Reasoning to develop ideas and connect claims to evidence
- Stylistic elements, such as word choice or appeals to emotion, to express ideas

When researchers and engineers undertake a large-scale scientific project, they may end up making discoveries and developing technologies that have far wider uses than originally intended. This is especially true in NASA, one of the most influential and innovative scientific organizations in America. NASA spinoff technology refers to innovations originally developed for NASA space projects that are now used in a wide range of different commercial fields. Many consumers are unaware that products they are buying are based on NASA research! Spinoff technology proves that it is worthwhile to invest in science research because it could enrich people's lives in unexpected ways.

The first spinoff technology worth mentioning is baby food. In space, where astronauts have limited access to fresh food and fewer options with their daily meals, malnutrition is a serious concern. Consequently, NASA researchers were looking for ways to enhance the nutritional value of astronauts' food. Scientists found that a certain type of algae could be added to food, improving the food's neurological benefits. When experts in the commercial food industry learned of this algae's potential to boost brain health, they were quick to begin their own research. The nutritional substance from algae then developed into a product called life's DHA, which can be found in over 90 percent of infant food sold in America.

Another intriguing example of a spinoff technology can be found in fashion. People who are always dropping their sunglasses may have invested in a pair of sunglasses with scratch resistant lenses—that is, it's impossible to scratch the glass, even if the glasses are dropped on an abrasive surface. This innovation is incredibly advantageous for people who are clumsy, but most shoppers don't know that this technology was originally developed by NASA. Scientists first created scratch resistant glass to help protect costly and crucial equipment from getting scratched in space, especially the helmet visors in space suits. However, sunglass companies later realized that this technology could be profitable for their products, and they licensed the technology from NASA.

Write an essay in which you explain how the author builds an argument to persuade the audience that it is worthwhile to invest in science research. In your essay, analyze how the author uses one or more of the features listed in the bullet points above (or features of your own choice) to strengthen the logic and persuasiveness of their argument. Focus on the most relevant features of the passage.

Reading Answers

1. D: Criticize a theory by presenting counterevidence. The author mentions anti-Stratfordian arguments in the first paragraph, but then goes on to debunk these theories with facts about Shakespeare's life in the second and third paragraphs. Choice *A* is incorrect because the author is far from unbiased; in fact, the author clearly disagrees with anti-Stratfordians. Choice *B* is also incorrect because it's more closely aligned with the beliefs of anti-Stratfordians. Choice *C* can be eliminated because, while it's true that the author gives historical background, the purpose is using that information to disprove a theory.

2. B: "But in fact, there isn't much substance to such speculation, and most anti-Stratfordian arguments can be refuted with a little background about Shakespeare's time and upbringing." The thesis is a statement that contains the author's topic and main idea. As seen in question 27, the purpose of this article is to use historical evidence to provide counterarguments to anti-Stratfordians. Choice *A* is simply a definition; Choice *C* is a supporting detail, not a main idea; and Choice *D* represents an idea of anti-Stratfordians, not the author's opinion.

3. C: Rhetorical question. A rhetorical question is asked not to obtain an answer but to encourage readers to more deeply consider an issue.

4. B: By explaining grade school curriculum in Shakespeare's time. This question asks readers to refer to the organizational structure of the article and demonstrate understanding of how the author provides details to support the argument. This particular detail can be found in the second paragraph: "even though he did not attend university, grade school education in Shakespeare's time was actually quite rigorous."

5. A: Busy. This is a vocabulary question that can be answered using context clues. Other sentences in the paragraph describe London as "the most populous city in England" filled with "crowds of people." Choice *B* is incorrect because London was in Shakespeare's home country, not a foreign one. Choice *C* isn't mentioned in the passage. Choice *D* isn't a good answer because the passage describes London as an important city, not underdeveloped.

6. D: In Shakespeare's time, glove-makers weren't part of the upper class. Anti-Stratfordians doubt Shakespeare's ability because he wasn't from the upper class; his father was a glove-maker; therefore, in at least this example, glove-makers weren't included in the upper class. This is an example of inductive reasoning, using two specific pieces of information to draw a more general conclusion.

7. C: It's an example of a play set outside of England. This detail comes from the third paragraph, where the author responds to skeptics who claim that Shakespeare wrote too much about places he never visited, so *Romeo and Juliet* is mentioned as a famous example of a play with a foreign setting. In order to answer this question, readers need to understand the author's purpose in the third paragraph and how the author uses details to support this purpose. Choices *A* and *D* aren't mentioned, and Choice *B* is clearly false because the passage mentions more than once that Shakespeare never left England.

8. A: It's possible to learn things from reading rather than firsthand experience. This inference can be made from the final paragraph, where the author refutes anti-Stratfordian skepticism by noting that books about life in Europe could circulate throughout London. From this statement, readers can conclude the author believes it's possible that Shakespeare learned about European culture from books. Choice *B* isn't true because the author believes that Shakespeare contributed to English literature without traveling extensively. Similarly, Choice *C* isn't a good answer because the author explains how

Shakespeare got his education without attending a university. Choice *D* can also be eliminated because the author describes Shakespeare's genius, and Shakespeare clearly isn't from Italy.

9. A: First person. This is a straightforward question that requires readers to know that a first-person narrator speaks from an "I" point of view.

10. D: He doesn't understand all of the languages being used. This can be inferred from the fact that the traveler must refer to his dictionary to understand those around him. Choice *A* isn't a good choice because the traveler seems to wonder why the driver needs to drive so fast. Choice *B* isn't mentioned in the passage and doesn't seem like a good answer choice because he seems wholly unfamiliar with his surroundings. This is why Choice *C* can also be eliminated.

11. B: From fearful to charmed. This can be found in the first sentence of the third paragraph, which states, "I soon lost sight and recollection of ghostly fears in the beauty of the scene as we drove along." Also, readers should get a sense of foreboding from the first two paragraphs, where superstitious villagers seem frightened on the traveler's behalf. However, the final paragraph changes to delighted descriptions of the landscape's natural beauty. Choices *A* and *D* can be eliminated because the traveler is anxious, not relaxed or comfortable at the beginning of the passage. Choice *C* can also be eliminated because the traveler doesn't gain any particular insights in the last paragraph, and in fact continues to lament that he cannot understand the speech of those around him.

12. D: A complete stranger. The answer to this reading comprehension question can be found in the second paragraph, when the traveler is "just starting for an unknown place to meet an unknown man"—in other words, a complete stranger.

13. C: The traveler will soon encounter danger or evil. Answering this prediction question requires readers to understand foreshadowing, or hints that the author gives about what will happen next. There are numerous hints scattered throughout this passage: the villager's sorrow and sympathy for the traveler and their superstitious actions; the spooky words that the traveler overhears; the driver's unexplained haste. All of these point to a danger that awaits the protagonist.

14. A: "I must say they weren't cheering to me, for amongst them were "Ordog"—Satan, "pokol"—hell, "stregoica"—witch, "vrolok" and "vlkoslak"—both of which mean the same thing, one being Slovak and the other Servian for something that is either were-wolf or vampire." As mentioned in question 13, this sentence is an example of how the author hints at evil to come for the traveler. The other answer choices aren't related to the passage's grim foreshadowing.

15. A: The purpose is to inform the reader about what assault is and how it is committed. Choice *B* is incorrect because the passage does not state that assault is a lesser form of lethal force, only that an assault can use lethal force, or alternatively, lethal force can be utilized to counter a dangerous assault. Choice *C* is incorrect because the passage is informative and does not have a set agenda. Finally, Choice *D* is incorrect because although the author uses an example in order to explain assault, it is not indicated that this is the author's personal account.

16. C: A man who is attacked in an alley by another man with a knife. If the man being attached used self-defense by lethal force, it would not be considered illegal. The presence of a deadly weapon indicates mal-intent and because the individual is isolated in an alley, lethal force in self-defense may be the only way to preserve his life. Choices *A* and *B* can be ruled out because in these situations, no one is in danger of immediate death or bodily harm by someone else. Choice *D* is an assault and does exhibit intent to harm, but this situation isn't severe enough to merit lethal force; there is no intent to kill.

17. B: As discussed in the second passage, there are several forms of assault, like assault with a deadly weapon, verbal assault, or threatening posture or language. Choice *A* is incorrect because lethal force and assault are separate as indicated by the passages. Choice *C* is incorrect because anyone is capable of assault; the author does not state that one group of people cannot commit assault. Choice *D* is incorrect because assault is never justified. Self-defense resulting in lethal force can be justified.

18. D: The use of lethal force is not evaluated on the intent of the user, but rather the severity of the primary attack that warranted self-defense. This statement most undermines the last part of the passage because it directly contradicts how the law evaluates the use of lethal force. Choices *A* and *B* are stated in the paragraph, and therefore do not undermine the explanation from the author. Choice *C* does not necessarily undermine the passage, but it does not support the passage either. It is more of an opinion that does not offer strength or weakness to the explanation.

19. C: An assault with deadly intent can lead to an individual using lethal force to preserve their well-being. Choice *C* is correct because it clearly establishes what both assault and lethal force are and gives the specific way in which the two concepts meet. Choice *A* is incorrect because lethal force doesn't necessarily result in assault. This is also why Choice *B* is incorrect. Not all assaults would necessarily be life threatening to the point where lethal force is needed for self-defense. Choice *D* is compelling but ultimately too vague; the statement touches on aspects of the two ideas but fails to present the concrete way in which the two are connected to each other.

20. A: Both passages open by defining a legal concept and then continue to describe situations in order to further explain the concept. Choice *D* is incorrect because while the passages utilize examples to help explain the concepts discussed, the author doesn't indicate that they are specific court cases. It's also clear that the passages don't open with examples, but instead begin by defining the terms addressed in each passage. This eliminates Choice *B* and ultimately reveals Choice *A* to be the correct answer. Choice *A* accurately outlines the way both passages are structured. Because the passages follow a near identical structure, the rest of the choices can easily be ruled out.

21. A: Intent is very important for determining both lethal force and assault; intent is examined in both parties and helps determine the severity of the issue. Choices *B* and *C* are incorrect because it is clear in both passages that intent is a prevailing theme in both lethal force and assault. Choice *D* is compelling, but if a person uses lethal force to defend themselves, the intent of the defender is also examined in order to help determine if there was excessive force used. Choice *A* is correct because it states that intent is important for determining both lethal force and assault, and that intent is used to gauge the severity of the issues. Remember, just as lethal force can escalate to excessive use of force, there are different kinds of assault. Intent dictates several different forms of assault.

22. B: To demonstrate a single example of two different types of assault, then adding in a third type of assault to the example's conclusion. The example mainly serves to show an instance of "threatening body language" and "provocative language" with the homeowner gesturing threats to his neighbor. It ends the example by adding a third type of assault: physical strikes. This example is used to show the variant nature of assaults. Choice *A* is incorrect because it doesn't mention the "physical strike" assault at the end and is not specific enough. Choice *C* is incorrect because the example does not say anything about the definition of lethal force or how it might be altered. Choice *D* is incorrect, as the example mentions nothing of cause and effect.

23. B: *Irrevocable* means irreversible or final. In its usage in the first passage, irrevocable damage remains that the damage is permanent and cannot be repaired. Choice *A* is an antonym and the other choices are unrelated to the definition.

24. B: Mr. Button's wife is about to have a baby. The passage begins by giving the reader information about traditional birthing situations. Then, we are told that Mr. and Mrs. Button decide to go against tradition to have their baby in a hospital. The next few passages are dedicated to letting the reader know how Mr. Button dresses and goes to the hospital to welcome his new baby. There is a doctor in this excerpt, as Choice *C* indicates, and Mr. Button does put on clothes, as Choice *D* indicates. However, Mr. Button is not going to the doctor's office nor is he about to go shopping for new clothes.

25. A: The tone of the above passage is nervous and excited. We are told in the fourth paragraph that Mr. Button "arose nervously." We also see him running without caution to the doctor to find out about his wife and baby—this indicates his excitement. We also see him stuttering in a nervous yet excited fashion as he asks the doctor if it's a boy or girl. Though the doctor may seem a bit abrupt at the end, indicating a bit of anger or shame, neither of these choices is the overwhelming tone of the entire passage.

26. C: Dedicated. Mr. Button is dedicated to the task before him. Choice *A*, numbed, Choice *B*, chained, and Choice *D*, moved, all could grammatically fit in the sentence. However, they are not synonyms with *consecrated* like Choice *C* is.

27. D: Giving readers a visual picture of what the doctor is doing. The author describes a visual image—the doctor rubbing his hands together—first and foremost. The author may be trying to make a comment about the profession; however, the author does not "explain the detail of the doctor's profession" as Choice *B* suggests.

28. D: To introduce the setting of the story and its characters. We know we are being introduced to the setting because we are given the year in the very first paragraph along with the season: "one day in the summer of 1860." This is a classic structure of an introduction of the setting. We are also getting a long explanation of Mr. Button, what his work is, who is related to him, and what his life is like in the third paragraph.

29. B: "Talk sense!" is an example of an imperative sentence. An imperative sentence gives a command. The doctor is commanding Mr. Button to talk sense. Choice *A* is an example of an exclamatory sentence, which expresses excitement. Choice *C* is an example of an interrogative sentence—these types of sentences ask questions. Choice *D* is an example of a declarative sentence. This means that the character is simply making a statement.

30. E: *Extraneous* most nearly means *superfluous*, or *trivial*. Choice *A*, *indispensable*, is incorrect because it means the opposite of *extraneous*. Choice *B*, *bewildering*, means *confusing* and is not relevant to the context of the sentence. Choice *C* is incorrect because *fallacious* means *false* or *wrong*. Finally, Choice *D* is wrong because although the prefix of the word is the same, *ex-*, the word *exuberant* means *elated* or *enthusiastic*, and is irrelevant to the context of the sentence.

31. A: This is a challenging question because the author's purpose is somewhat open-ended. The author concludes by stating that the questions regarding human perception and observation can be approached from many angles. Thus, the author does not seem to be attempting to prove one thing or another. Choice B is incorrect because we cannot know for certain whether the electron experiment is the latest discovery in astroparticle physics because no date is given. Choice *C* is a broad generalization that does not reflect accurately on the writer's views. While the author does appear to reflect on opposing views of human understanding (Choice *D*), the best answer is Choice *A*. Choice *E* is also wrong because the author never says that classical philosophy is wrong or directly attempts to debunk it.

32. C: It presents a problem, explains the details of that problem, and then ends with more inquiry. The beginning of this paragraph literally "presents a conundrum," explains the problem of partial understanding, and then ends with more questions, or inquiry. There is no solution offered in this paragraph, making Choices *A, B,* and *E* incorrect. Choice *D* is incorrect because the paragraph does not begin with a definition.

33. D: Looking back in the text, the author describes that classical philosophy holds that understanding can be reached by careful observation. This will not work if they are overly invested or biased in their pursuit. Choices *A*, *B*, and *C* are in no way related and are completely unnecessary. A specific theory is not necessary to understanding, according to classical philosophy mentioned by the author. Again, the key to understanding is observing the phenomena outside of it, without biased or predisposition. Thus, Choice *E* is wrong.

34. B: The electrons passed through both holes and then onto the plate. Choices *A*, *C*, and *E* are wrong because such movement is not mentioned at all in the text. In the passage, the author says that electrons that were physically observed appeared to pass through one hole or another. Remember, the electrons that were observed doing this were described as acting like particles. Therefore, Choice *D* is wrong. Recall that the plate actually recorded electrons passing through both holes simultaneously and hitting the plate. This behavior—the electron activity that wasn't seen by humans—was characteristic of waves. Thus, Choice *B* is the right answer.

35. C: The author uses "gravity" to demonstrate an example of natural phenomena humans discovered and understand without the use of tools or machines. Choice *A* mirrors the language in the beginning of the paragraph but is incorrect in its intent. Choice *B* is incorrect; the paragraph mentions nothing of "not knowing the true nature of gravity." Choices *D* and *E* are both incorrect as well. There is no mention of an "alternative solution" or "looking forward" to new technology in this paragraph.

36. E: The important thing to keep in mind is that we must choose a scenario that best parallels, or is most similar to, the discovery of the experiment mentioned in the passage. The important aspects of the experiment can be summed up like so: humans directly observed one behavior of electrons and then through analyzing a tool (the plate that recorded electron hits), discovered that there was another electron behavior that could not be physically seen by human eyes. This best mirrors the scenario in Choice *E*. Like Feynman, the colorblind person is able to observe one aspect of the world but through the special goggles (a tool) he is able to see a natural phenomenon that he could not physically see on his own. While Choice *D* is compelling because an x-ray helps humans see the broken bone, it is not necessarily revealing that the bone is broken in the first place. The other choices do not parallel the scenario in question. Therefore, Choice *E* is the best choice.

37. B: The author would not agree that technology renders human observation irrelevant. Choice *A* is incorrect because much of the passage discusses how technology helps humans observe what cannot be seen with the naked eye; therefore, the author would agree with this statement. This line of reasoning is also why the author would agree with Choice *D*, making it incorrect as well. As indicated in the second paragraph, the author seems to think that humans create inventions and tools with the goal of studying phenomena more precisely. This indicates increased understanding as people recognize limitations and develop items to help bypass the limitations and learn. Therefore, Choice *C* is incorrect as well. Again, the author doesn't attempt to disprove or dismiss classical philosophy. He or she actually offers examples of how classical understanding is still used in the world, such as the gravity example. Therefore, the author would agree with Choice *E*.

38. E: The author explains that Boethianism is a Medieval theological philosophy that attributes sin to temporary pleasure and righteousness with virtue and God's providence. Besides Choice *E,* the choices listed are all physical things. While these could still be divine rewards, Boethianism holds that the true reward for being virtuous is in God's favor. It is also stressed in the article that physical pleasures cannot be taken into the afterlife. Therefore, the best choice is *E*, God's favor.

39. C: *The Canterbury Tales* presents a manuscript written in the medieval period that can help illustrate Boethianism through stories and show how people of the time might have responded to the idea. Choices *A* and *B* are generalized statements, and we have no evidence to support Choice *B.* There is also no evidence that Chaucer was a devoted Boethianist, so Choice *E* is wrong. Choice *D* is very compelling, but it looks at Boethianism in a way that the author does not. The author does not mention "different levels of Boethianism" when discussing the tales, only that the concept appears differently in different tales. Boethianism also doesn't focus on enlightenment.

40. D: The author is referring to the principle that a desire for material goods leads to moral malfeasance punishable by a higher being. Choice *A* is incorrect; while the text does mention thieves ravaging others' possessions, it is only meant as an example and not as the principle itself. Choice *B* is incorrect for the same reason as Choice *A*. Choice *C* is mentioned in the text and is part of the example that proves the principle, and also not the principle itself. Choice *E* might be something the author holds to be true; however, it is not the main principle laid out in the two examples.

41. C: The word *avarice* most nearly means *parsimoniousness*, or an unwillingness to spend money. Choice *A* means *evil* or *mischief* and does not relate to the context of the sentence. Choice *B* is also incorrect, because *pithiness* means *shortness* or *conciseness.* Choice *D*, *pompousness*, means someone is arrogant, which is also irrelevant to the context of the sentence. Choice *E* is close because *precariousness* means dangerous or unstable, which goes well with the context. However, we are told of the summoner's specific characteristic of greed, which makes Choice *C* the best answer.

42. D: Desire for pleasure can lead toward sin. Boethianism acknowledges desire as something that leads out of holiness, so Choice *A* is incorrect. Choice *B* is incorrect because in the passage, Boethianism is depicted as being wary of desire and anything that binds people to the physical world. Choices *C* and *E* can be eliminated because the author never says that desire indicates demonic possession or that it is the result of original sin.

43. C: In lines 6 and 7, it is stated that avarice can prevent a man from being necessitously poor, but too timorous, or fearful, to achieve real wealth. According to the passage, avarice does tend to make a person very wealthy. The passage states that oppression, not avarice, is the consequence of wealth. The passage does not state that avarice drives a person's desire to be wealthy.

44. D: Paine believes that the distinction that is beyond a natural or religious reason is between king and subjects. He states that the distinction between good and bad is made in heaven. The distinction between male and female is natural. He does not mention anything about the distinction between humans and animals.

45. A: The passage states that the Heathens were the first to introduce government by kings into the world. The quiet lives of patriarchs came before the Heathens introduced this type of government. It was Christians, not Heathens, who paid divine honors to living kings. Heathens honored deceased kings. Equal rights of nature are mentioned in the paragraph, but not in relation to the Heathens.

46. B: Paine asserts that a monarchy is against the equal rights of nature and cites several parts of scripture that also denounce it. He doesn't say it is against the laws of nature. Because he uses scripture to further his argument, it is not despite scripture that he denounces the monarchy. Paine addresses the law by saying the courts also do not support a monarchical government.

47. A: To be *idolatrous* is to worship idols or heroes, in this case, kings. It is not defined as being deceitful. While idolatry is considered a sin, it is an example of a sin, not a synonym for it. Idolatry may have been considered illegal in some cultures, but it is not a definition for the term.

48. A: The essential meaning of the passage is that the Almighty, God, would disapprove of this type of government. While heaven is mentioned, it is done so to suggest that the monarchical government is irreverent, not that heaven isn't promised. God's disapproval is mentioned, not his punishment. The passage refers to the Jewish monarchy, which required both belief in God and kings.

49. D: This is the correct answer choice because expository writing involves straightforward, factual information and analysis. It is unbiased and does not rely on the writer's personal feelings or opinions. Choice *A* is incorrect because narrative writing tells a story. Choice *B* is incorrect because persuasive writing is intended to change the reader's mind or position on a topic. Choice *C* is incorrect because technical writing attempts to outline a complex object or process.

50. B: This is the correct answer choice because the passage begins by describing Carver's childhood fascination with painting and later returns to this point when it states that at the end of his career "Carver returned to his first love of art." For this reason, all the other answer choices are incorrect.

51. A: This is the correct answer choice because the passage contains a definition of the term, *agricultural monoculture*, which is very similar to this answer.

52. C: This is the correct answer choice because there is ample evidence in the passage that refers to Carver's brilliance and the fact that his discoveries had a far-reaching impact both then and now. There is no evidence in the passage to support any of the other answer choices.

Writing and Language Answers

1. B: Move the sentence so that it comes before the preceding sentence. For this question, place the underlined sentence in each prospective choice's position. To keep as-is is incorrect because the father "going crazy" doesn't logically follow the fact that he was a "city slicker." Choice *C* is incorrect because the sentence in question is not a concluding sentence and does not transition smoothly into the second paragraph. Choice *D* is incorrect because the sentence doesn't necessarily need to be omitted since it logically follows the very first sentence in the passage.

2. D: Choice *D* is correct because "As it turns out" indicates a contrast from the previous sentiment, that the RV was a great purchase. Choice *A* is incorrect because the sentence needs an effective transition from the paragraph before. Choice *B* is incorrect because the text indicates it *is* surprising that the RV was a great purchase because the author was skeptical beforehand. Choice *C* is incorrect because the transition "Furthermore" does not indicate a contrast.

3. B: This sentence calls for parallel structure. Choice *B* is correct because the verbs "wake," "eat," and "break" are consistent in tense and parts of speech. Choice *A* is incorrect because the words "wake" and "eat" are present tense while the word "broke" is in past tense. Choice *C* is incorrect because this turns the sentence into a question, which doesn't make sense within the context. Choice *D* is incorrect because it breaks tense with the rest of the passage. "Waking," "eating," and "breaking" are all present participles, and the context around the sentence is in past tense.

4. C: Choice *C* is correct because it is clear, concise, and fits within the context of the passage. Choice *A* is incorrect because "We rejoiced as 'hackers'" does not give reason *why* hacking was rejoiced. Choice *B* is incorrect because it does not mention a solution being found and is therefore not specific enough. Choice *D* is incorrect because the meaning is eschewed by the helping verb "had to rejoice," and the sentence does not give enough detail as to what the problem entails.

5. A: The original sentence is correct because the verb tense as well as the order of the sentence makes sense in the given context. Choice *B* is incorrect because the order of the words makes the sentence more confusing than it otherwise would be. Choice *C* is incorrect because "We are even making" is in present tense. Choice *D* is incorrect because "We will make" is future tense. The surrounding text of the sentence is in past tense.

6. B: Choice *B* is correct because there is no punctuation needed if a dependent clause ("while traveling across America") is located behind the independent clause ("it allowed us to share adventures"). Choice *A* is incorrect because there are two dependent clauses connected and no independent clause, and a complete sentence requires at least one independent clause. Choice *C* is incorrect because of the same reason as Choice *A*. Semicolons have the same function as periods: there must be an independent clause on either side of the semicolon. Choice *D* is incorrect because the dash simply interrupts the complete sentence.

7. C: The rules for "me" and "I" is that one should use "I" when it is the subject pronoun of a sentence, and "me" when it is the object pronoun of the sentence. Break the sentence up to see if "I" or "me" should be used. To say "Those are memories that I have now shared" makes more sense than to say "Those are memories that me have now shared." Choice *D* is incorrect because "my siblings" should come before "I."

8. B: Choice *B* is correct. Here, a colon is used to introduce an explanation. Colons either introduce explanations or lists. Additionally, the quote ends with the punctuation inside the quotes, unlike Choice *C*.

9. A: The verb tense in this passage is predominantly in the present tense, so Choice *A* is the correct answer. Choice *B* is incorrect because the subject and verb do not agree. It should be "Education provides," not "Education provide." Choice *C* is incorrect because the passage is in present tense, and "Education will provide" is future tense. Choice *D* doesn't make sense when placed in the sentence.

10. D: The possessive form of the word "it" is "its." The contraction "it's" denotes "it is." Thus, Choice *A* is wrong. The word "raises" in Choice *B* makes the sentence grammatically incorrect. Choice *C* adds an apostrophe at the end of "its." While adding an apostrophe to most words would indicate possession, adding *'s* to the word "it" indicates a contraction.

11. C: The word *civilised* should be spelled *civilized.* The words "distinguishes" and "creatures" are both spelled correctly.

12. B: Choice *B* is correct because it provides clarity by describing what "myopic" means right after the word itself. Choice *A* is incorrect because the explanation of "myopic" comes before the word; thus, the meaning is skewed. It's possible that Choice *C* makes sense within context. However, it's not the *best* way to say this. Choice *D* is confusingly worded. Using "myopic focus" is not detrimental to society; however, the way *D* is worded makes it seem so.

13. C: Again, we see where the second paragraph can be divided into two parts due to separate topics. The first section's main focus is education addressing the mind, body, and soul. The first section, then, could end with the concluding sentence, "The human heart and psyche . . ." The next sentence to start a new paragraph would be "Education is a basic human right." The rest of this paragraph talks about what education is and some of its characteristics.

14. A: Choice *A* is correct because the phrase "others' ideas" is both plural and indicates possession. Choice *B* is incorrect because "other's" indicates only one "other" that's in possession of "ideas," which is incorrect. Choice *C* is incorrect because no possession is indicated. Choice *D* is incorrect because the word "other" does not end in *s*. *Others's* is not a correct form of the word in any situation.

15. D: This sentence must have a comma before "although" because the word "although" is connecting two independent clauses. Thus, Choices *B* and *C* are incorrect. Choice *A* is incorrect because the second sentence in the underlined section is a fragment.

16. C: Choice *C* is the correct choice because the word "their" indicates possession, and the text is talking about "their students," or the students of someone. Choice *A*, "there," means at a certain place and is incorrect. Choice *B*, "they're," is a contraction and means "they are." Choice *D* is not a word.

17. B: Choice *B* uses all punctuation correctly in this sentence. In American English, single quotes should only be used if they are quotes within a quote, making choices *A* and *C* incorrect. Additionally, punctuation here should go inside the quotes, making Choice *D* incorrect.

18. B: Choice *B* is correct because the conjunction "and" is used to connect phrases that are to be used jointly, such as teachers working hard to help students "identify salient information" and to "think critically." The conjunctions *so*, *but*, and *nor* are incorrect in the context of this sentence.

19. A: Choice *A* has consistent parallel structure with the verbs "read," "identify," and "determine." Choices *B* and *C* have faulty parallel structure with the words "determining" and "identifying." Choice *D* has incorrect subject/verb agreement. The sentence should read, "Students have to read . . . identify . . . and determine."

20. D: The correct choice for this sentence is that "they are . . . shaped by the influences." The prepositions "for," "to," and "with" do not make sense in this context. People are *shaped by*, not *shaped for, shaped to,* or *shaped with*.

21. A: To see which answer is correct, it might help to place the subject, "Teachers," near the verb. Choice *A* is correct: "Teachers . . . must strive" makes grammatical sense here. Choice *B* is incorrect because "Teachers . . . to strive" does not make grammatical sense. Choice *C* is incorrect because "Teachers must not only respect . . . but striving" eschews parallel structure. Choice *D* is incorrect because it is in past tense, and this passage is in present tense.

22. C: Choice *C* is correct because it uses an em-dash. Em-dashes are versatile. They can separate phrases that would otherwise be in parenthesis, or they can stand in for a colon. In this case, a colon would be another decent choice for this punctuation mark because the second sentence expands upon the first sentence. Choice *A* is incorrect because the statement is not a question. Choice *B* is incorrect because adding a comma here would create a comma splice. Choice *D* is incorrect because this creates a run-on sentence since the two sentences are independent clauses.

23. C: While the text is clearly informative, there is a definite goal in the writing. The author is presenting evidence and key information to illustrate a specific point. Choice *A* is incorrect. Choices *B* and *D* are also incorrect because the author does not mention or directly state any of these things, but instead focuses on Odysseus' experiences and how, and why, they have shaped his character. This makes *C* the correct answer, which can also be seen clearly laid out in the first paragraph.

24. A: "However" is an appropriate word to begin this sentence since it illustrates the idea of contrast: some of the female Odysseus encountered were helpful, *however* some were clearly not. Therefore, we can eliminate Choice *D*. Choice *B* is also wrong because it eliminates the word "several", which is also useful in distinguishing that, while some female characters were benevolent, several were deceptive and even harmful. Choice *C* is wrong because it lacks the comma after "However". Thus, this part of the sentence requires no edits, making the choice *A,* NO CHANGE.

25. D: This portion of the sentence could certainly use revision, but one aspect that should definitely remain is the use of a comma in the structure. Eliminating the comma in this portion of the sentence will make the sentence a run-on and confuse the reader. A comma is needed to link these two ideas together, which makes choice *B* easy to eliminate. For this reason, Choice *C* can also be ruled out. Even with the word "which" added for clarity, a comma is still necessary for the overall construction. Choice *D* has several very good modifications that both maintain the original meaning of the sentence and make it easier to read. In Choice *D,* the comma is included. Another good modification is eliminating *himself,* which is confusing and unnecessary. Changing "it forces" to "forcing" also makes the sentence clearer and eliminates word cluster. All these factors make *D* the correct answer, which means that Choice *A* wrong.

26. D: All of the answer choices are correct. Quotes from the original text serve to enlighten the reader about specific moments and context within the work, illustrate where the author gets their ideas, and also cite examples as evidence. The author does all of these things with the quotes, making *D* the correct answer. Be sure to read such questions carefully and consider how an author uses additional materials in the passage, such as quotes or graphs.

27. A: Choice *D* is wrong, *concealing* is the improper tense and it throws off the sentence. Choice *B* is a very good possibility, but the "be" is ultimately unnecessary in the context of the sentence, so it can be eliminated. Choice *C* is also very tempting because "concealed" would fit into the sentence, but it isn't as strong as the original "to conceal". This is so because "to conceal" suggests the active of use the word towards an objective. "Odysseus had concealed himself" is more passive than "Odysseus had to conceal". The latter suggests a more direct action, which is what the author is trying to communicate. This makes choice *A,* NO CHANGE, the best option.

28. C: Choice *D* can be ruled out. While this shorter option makes for a quicker transition into the next sentence, it does not convey the full depth of what the writer is trying to communicate. Sometimes shorter sentences are not always the answer! What will be the correct answer is a sentence that flows and communicates the message of the original sentence more effectively and with correct punctuation. Choice *A* can quickly be dismissed because of its grammatical errors and lack of necessary punctuation. Choice *B* seems to retain most of the same diction of the original sentence, but Choice *C* is more direct and better phrased. Choice *C* also gives the reader a better impression of how important hospitality is in context of the story and culture. Another note: in the original sentence, there needed to be a comma after "dwelling", but Choice *C* fixes this with commas after "hospitality" and "instead".

29. B: *Relinquishes* means to give up or to voluntarily cease control of something. This is not something Odysseus does because he does not surrender his true name, he just hides it, metaphorically becoming someone else. Choice *A* is wrong. Therefore, Choice *B, conceals,* is the best option because Odysseus does in fact hide (or conceal) his true identity behind a false name. He does not *withhold* (Choice *C*) his true identity but offers an alternative. Choice *D* is synonymous with *relinquishes* and therefore, it is also wrong.

30. A: Reading through the sentence, one can see that it flows and uses proper punctuation and grammar, which means that Choice *A* is the correct answer. Choice *B* lacks the necessary comma after "Clearly", making it incorrect. Choice *C* utilizes an unnecessary semicolon. Choice *D* makes the sentence awkward by placing *clearly* in the middle of the sentence.

31. D: The opening passage basically sums up that Odysseus's distrust of women and those seeming to have honorable intentions can be attributed to the experiences he faced when trying to return to home to Ithaca. This distrust is something the author argues was developed through multiple experiences, not that Odysseus was naturally distrustful. While Odysseus' cleverness is what gets him through the trials he faced, this isn't what the author focused on in the passage. This makes Choice *D* the strongest answer.

32. B: Choice B is the best answer because it avoids the wordiness of the original phrase also like, which makes Choice A incorrect. Choice C is compelling, but it lacks the necessary information that the original sentence has: we need to have Polyphemus still in the sentence. Choice D is a decent option, but much of it is unnecessary and already addressed in the remainder of the sentence that isn't underlined.

33. B: The issue with this word is that it lacks proper punctuation. "One" is referring to an individual, and it needs to show possession of "identity". Therefore, *ones* must have an apostrophe to show ownership and to be correct. Thus, choice *B one's*, is the correct answer.

34. C: The current phrase seems to repeat itself, and really refers more to beginning something rather than an arrival, so we can eliminate Choice *A*. Choices *B* and *D* are compelling but are somewhat specific. What must be communicated is that all men who reach the island, in whatever fashion, risked being seduced by Circe. Choice *C* is the most practical revision and is more direct, while allowing for other circumstances in which men come to Circe's island. In the end, "arrive on" also sounds better when plugged into the sentence.

35. B: The best answer is Choice B, ensure, which means to make certain. Odysseus is trying to make certain that he and the crew will be safe by beating Circe at her own game. Choice A, assure, means to speak to someone in a way that eliminates doubt. This indirectly relates to what Odysseus wants to do, but to assure specifically refers to speaking to someone. Choices C and D are totally irrelevant. Vindicate means to free from blame, while prevent means to stop from happening.

36. B: Without this sentence, the reader must infer the connection between the two characters. It is better to let the short sentence remain to ensure that the reader will understand parallels between the two characters: both sought to return home, but when one did, his wife betrayed him. This is the primary reason for keeping the sentence, making Choice *B* the answer.

37. A: Changing the main construction of this section of the sentence will throw off the entire sentence. There must be a comma in place in order to separate ideas in this particularly long, but correct, sentence. The way the author has already laid out this section of the sentence already laid out is correct therefore Choice *A*, NO CHANGE, is right.

38. A: There should be no change here. Both underlined sentences are complete and do not need changing. Choice *B* is incorrect because since there is no punctuation between the two independent clauses, it is considered a run-on. Choice *C* is incorrect because placing a comma between two independent clauses creates a comma splice. Choice *D* is incorrect. The underlined portion could *possibly* act with a colon. However, it's not the best choice, so omit Choice *D*.

39. D: Choice *D* is correct. The text before this underlined phrase talks about the difference between "discovery" and "exploration," so making a decision on what term to label Columbus would be the best choice. The other three choices may be true to the historical narrative of Columbus; however, they do not fit within the surrounding text.

40. B: This question seeks to determine the best introductory word for the main point of the following sentence. Choice *B* is correct; the word "Rather" indicates something unexpected. "Rather" fits in this sentence because it is "unexpected" that Leif Erikson first came to the New World and not Columbus. Choice *A* is incorrect; "Nevertheless" means "all the same," and does not fit with the sentiment of this sentence. Choice *C* is incorrect because "Finally" is used to indicate the last point in a series, and we do not have a listed series here. The word "Suddenly" is used to indicate something that has happened quickly or unexpectedly. Thus, Choice *D* is incorrect.

41. C: Choice *C* is correct; the underlined phrase consists of part of an independent clause and a dependent clause ("Depending on which historian you seek.") The dependent clause cannot stand by itself. Thus, the best choice is to connect the two clauses with a comma. Choices *A* and *D* do not work because you must have two independent clauses on either side of a period as well as a semicolon. Choice *B* is incorrect because an exclamation point is used to show excitement and does not fit the tone here.

42. A: There should be no change. The sentence fits perfectly before the current one because in question is who raised Leif. Choice *B* is incorrect because this narrative is in chronological order, and by the end of the second paragraph, Leif is already an adult. Choice *C* wouldn't work because the sentence is not an introductory sentence. Rather, it shares the details of Leif's childhood. Finally, Choice *D* is incorrect because there is already a transition, "Instead," to lead into the next sentence.

43. C: To find out the best answer, try out each answer choice. Choice *A* is incorrect; it might make sense that Leif is "later trying to return home." However, the next sentence says "Leif with the intention of taking supplies," and is not grammatically correct. Choice *B* is also incorrect because we would have the same problem with "Leif with the intention of taking supplies." Choice *D* is not a good answer choice because it inverts words that are otherwise clear with Choice *C*, "Leif later tried to return home with the intention of taking supplies."

44. B: The most appropriate verb for this sentence is Choice *B*, "Leif consulted." Choice *A* is in present tense and therefore does not fit with the rest of the passage. Choice *C* is incorrect because "consulting" is present progressive tense and also does not fit with the consistent past tense of the passage. Choice *D*, "Leif was consulted with a merchant," doesn't make sense. Leif can consult with a merchant or be consulted *by* a merchant.

Dear SAT Test Taker,

We would like to start by thanking you for purchasing this study guide for your SAT exam. We hope that we exceeded your expectations.

Our goal in creating this study guide was to cover all of the topics that you will see on the test. We also strove to make our practice questions as similar as possible to what you will encounter on test day. With that being said, if you found something that you feel was not up to your standards, please send us an email and let us know.

We would also like to let you know about other books in our catalog that may interest you.

SAT

This can be found on Amazon: amazon.com/dp/1628455217

ACT

amazon.com/dp/1628454709

SAT Math 1

amazon.com/dp/1628454717

ACCUPLACER

amazon.com/dp/162845492X

TSI

amazon.com/dp/162845511X

AP Biology

amazon.com/dp/1628454989

We have study guides in a wide variety of fields. If the one you are looking for isn't listed above, then try searching for it on Amazon or send us an email.

Thanks Again and Happy Testing!
Product Development Team
info@studyguideteam.com

Interested in buying more than 10 copies of our product? Contact us about bulk discounts:

bulkorders@studyguideteam.com

FREE Test Taking Tips DVD Offer

To help us better serve you, we have developed a Test Taking Tips DVD that we would like to give you for FREE. **This DVD covers world-class test taking tips that you can use to be even more successful when you are taking your test.**

All that we ask is that you email us your feedback about your study guide. Please let us know what you thought about it – whether that is good, bad or indifferent.

To get your **FREE Test Taking Tips DVD**, email freedvd@studyguideteam.com with "FREE DVD" in the subject line and the following information in the body of the email:

a. The title of your study guide.

b. Your product rating on a scale of 1-5, with 5 being the highest rating.

c. Your feedback about the study guide. What did you think of it?

d. Your full name and shipping address to send your free DVD.

If you have any questions or concerns, please don't hesitate to contact us at freedvd@studyguideteam.com.

Thanks again!

57590715R00093

Made in the USA
Middletown, DE
01 August 2019